Good Health
Low Fat   Low Sodium
CLAY POT
COOKBOOK

– Hedi Levine –

TRIPART

Library of Congress Cataloging-in-Publication Data

Levine, Hedi
    The good health, low-fat, low-sodium clay pot cookbook / by Hedi Levine
        p.   cm.
    ISBN 1-882606-58-2
        1. Clay pot cookery.   2. Low-fat diet – Recipes   3. Salt-free diet – Recipes.
I. Title.
TX825 . 5 . L48   1996
641 . 5 ' 89 – dc20   96-1167
                                                                       CIP

TRIPART, LTD.
118 East 25th Street, New York, NY 10010
1275 Fanning Road, New Suffolk, NY 11956

Publisher: George Wieser
Creative Director: Tony Meisel
Editor: Sarah May Clarkson
Composition: Diane Specioso
Origination: Emirates Printing Press

Impreso por Printer Colombiana S.A.
Impreso en Colombia — Printed in Colombia

ISBN 1-882606-58-2

CONTENTS

INTRODUCTION

Cooking in an unglazed, wet, terra-cotta clay pot is an ancient tradition that dates back to the Etruscans; it also turns out to be a solution to many of the dietary issues that concern cooks today. Because of the unique characteristics of wet-clay heat, cooks need not add fat and excessive salt to their preparations in order to impart intense and satisfying flavor to the results. The concentrated moist heat of the clay pot does that. And, because for the most part, food cooks unattended once the clay cooker is closed, time-pressed cooks can use the intervening time in any way their schedule demands.

Though clay pot cooking is not labor intensive, it does require simple advance planning: the clay pot must be soaked for 10 to 15 minutes before it is filled and placed in the oven. Stews and small cuts of meat can be ready in as little as 45 minutes while whole chickens and large cuts of meat require about twice as much time.

The simplest combinations of meat or poultry layered with coarsely chopped savory flavorings and vegetables – onions, garlic, carrots or soft vegetables such as zucchini or tomatoes, perhaps a splash of wine – yield a full meal complete with complex sauce. By varying the components, the cook can invent unlimited variations. To switch a dish from Italian to Thai a cook can simply substitute ginger, coconut milk and lemon grass for olives, capers and tomatoes. The recipes in this book will give the basics: techniques, proportions, temperature and timing.

WHAT YOU NEED TO KNOW

SOAKING
Always submerge the top and bottom of the clay pot in water for at least 10 to 15 minutes before filling and cooking. It is the water that the unglazed pot absorbs during this soaking that creates the moist cooking atmosphere unique to clay pot cooking. The moist atmosphere eliminates the need for additional fat for basic cooking.

TEMPERATURE
Never expose a clay pot to sudden changes in temperature. It may crack.

Always place your filled clay pot in a cold oven. Never preheat. For an electric oven, set the oven temperature and turn it on when you put the pot into the oven. For a gas oven, select an intermediate temperature for the first five minutes, then set the oven to the appropriate temperature.

Do not pour boiling liquid into a cold clay pot or very cold liquid into a hot clay pot. This can cause it to crack.

Do not place a hot clay pot on a cold wet surface or expose a clay pot to direct heat – on top of the stove, on a grill or under a broiler.

TIMES AND OVEN SETTINGS
Use a very high temperature – at least 400°F, but usually 450°F to 480°F degrees. The high heat turns the moisture in the pot to steam and the clay pot insulates the food from the high temperatures. Use the times in the recipes as a guide, but adjust times and temperatures depending upon your oven. Because food cooks slowly within a covered clay pot, food will not overcook in a matter of minutes. However, when you remove the lid for browning, at the end of cooking, keep a close check.

THE CLAY POT PROCESS

To get the most out of your clay pot, note that the placement of herbs and aromatic vegetables can intensify their flavor during cooking. Many recipes call for a bottom layer of onions and aromatic vegetables; and herbs should be tucked beneath cuts of meat or between layers so that the moisture can release the flavors and infuse the meat or poultry.

   Although the sugars in meats and vegetables will carmelize (and brown) as they cook in a clay pot, to promote a crisper texture the lid should be removed at the end of cooking. Because of the high oven temperatures, watch your food carefully to avoid overcooking at this stage.

CLEANING AND STORING

Check your manufacturer's instructions to prepare your clay pot for first use. Generally, scrub it with a stiff brush and hot water and rinse well. For routine cleaning, limit the use of dishwashing soap. Instead, use very hot water mixed with baking soda, and scrub with a stiff brush. Don't worry if the clay pot changes color over time, darkening with use. However, if the clay pot becomes heavily soiled or stained, or if you want to remove the odors of particular dish (like fish or curry), a more involved cleaning is in order.

Soak the pot for several hours or overnight. Pour off the soaking water and add fresh cold water with baking soda or baking soda and vinegar mixed. Place the clay pot in a cold oven and set the temperature to 350°F for 30 minutes, raising the oven temperature to 450°F for an additional 40 to 60 minutes. After the pot has cooled for 15 minutes, scrub the inside of the pot gently with a scrub brush; dump the dirty water and rinse with clean hot water.

Always allow your washed clay pot to dry completely before putting it away. Store with the lid inverted inside the pot; allowing air to curculate keeps the pot fresh. Should your pot develop a moldy or rancid odor, clean it thoroughly with baking soda and water. Never stack other pots and pans on top of the clay pot as this can cause chips and cracks.

With these simple rules, the world of clay pot cooking is open to you. Enjoy the discoveries that will enrich this satisfying cooking technique, and enjoy the food with family and friends.

NOTE

All the recipes can be cooked in the regular Romertopf® pots or the specialized pots which are available. Choose a pot with the closest capacity. For your guidance, the 3 quart pot is the Romertopf® 111 model. The 4 quart pot is the Romertopf® 113 model. All recipes and pot sizes contain metric equivalents in parentheses.

SOUPS

SOUPE BONNE FEMME

½ tbs (8 ml) butter
1 tbs (15 ml) oil
1 lb (455 g) leeks, sliced
1½ lbs (685 g) potatoes, diced
1 tbs (15 ml) all-purpose flour
2 cups (480 ml) defatted low-sodium chicken stock
salt, optional
pepper, optional
1 bay leaf
2 sprigs tarragon
    or 1 tsp (5 ml) dried tarragon
2 cups (480 ml) skim milk

Soak the top and the bottom of 3-quart (3 l) clay pot in water for 10 minutes; drain.

Heat the butter and oil in a large nonstick saucepan. Reserve a few pieces of leek for garnish. Add the remaining leeks and potatoes, then cook, stirring, for about 5 minutes, until the leeks are slightly softened. Stir in the flour, then pour in the stock, stirring all the time.

Transfer the leek and potato mixture to the soaked clay pot. Add seasoning, bay leaf and tarragon. Cover the clay pot and place in the cold oven. Set the oven at 400°F (205°C). Cook for 50 minutes. Gradually stir the milk into the soup. Cook, covered, for another 40 minutes, until the vegetables are tender.

Serve the soup either chunky or processed until smooth in a blender. Taste for seasoning before serving; garnish with the reserved leek. Serves 4.

Approximate nutritional analysis per serving:
Calories 321, Protein 9 g, Carbohydrates 59 g, Fat 6 g, Saturated Fat 2 g,
16% of Calories from Fat, Cholesterol 6 mg, Sodium 1 mg

Gradually stir the milk into the soup.

ANGLO-INDIAN MULLIGATAWNY

1 tbs (15 ml) olive oil
2 onions, chopped
1 garlic clove, crushed
1 potato, diced
2 carrots, diced
2 tbs (30 ml) ground coriander
1 tbs (15 ml) cumin seeds
6 cardamom pods
1 bay leaf
½ lb (233 g) red lentils
salt, optional
pepper, to taste
5 ⅔ cups (1.5 l) defatted low-sodium chicken stock
4 tbs (60 ml) low-fat plain yogurt
chopped cilantro, to garnish

Soak the top and the bottom of 3-quart (3 l) clay pot in water for 10 minutes; drain.

Heat the oil in a saucepan. Add the onions, garlic, potato and carrots, and cook for 10 minutes, stirring all the time, until the onion is slightly softened. Stir in the coriander and cumin and cook for 2 minutes, then turn the mixture into the soaked clay pot. Add the cardamom pods, bay leaf and lentils. Sprinkle in seasoning, mix well, then stir in the stock.

Cover the clay pot and place in the cold oven. Set the oven at 400°F (205°C). Cook for 1½-2 hours, stirring once. The lentils should be cooked until mushy, so that they thicken the soup, and the vegetables should be very tender.

Taste for seasoning, then serve each portion topped with a little yogurt and sprinkled with cilantro leaves. Serves 4.

Approximate nutritional analysis per serving:
Calories 387, Protein 26 g, Carbohydrates 58 g, Fat 6 g, Saturated Fat 1 g,
15% of Calories from Fat, Cholesterol 1 mg, Sodium 52 mg

Add the cardamom pods, bay leaf and lentils.

HERBED ZUCCHINI SOUP

4 slices bacon, coarsely chopped
6-8 medium zucchini (2 ½ lbs [1.1 kg]),
cut into ½-inch (1.5 cm) slices
1 medium onion, chopped
1 small clove garlic, cut into slivers
1 ¼ cups (295 ml) defatted homemade beef broth
2 ½ cups (590 ml) water
¼ cup (60 ml) minced fresh parsley
1 tsp (5 ml) dried basil leaves
½ tsp (3 ml) salt
⅛ tsp (.5 ml) pepper
6 tsp (30 ml) grated Parmesan cheese

Soak top and bottom of 3-qt (3 l) clay pot in water about 10 minutes; drain.

Place bacon pieces in clay pot. Place covered clay pot in a cold oven. Set oven at 450°F (230°C). Bake, stirring once or twice, until bacon is light brown, 20-25 minutes.

Pour off and discard drippings. Add remaining ingredients except cheese. Reduce oven temperature to 400°F (205°C). Bake covered until zucchini is tender, about 40 minutes.

Process mixture, about 2 cups at a time, in blender or food processor until smooth. Return mixture to clay pot; bake covered until very hot, about 10 minutes.

Sprinkle cheese over each serving. Serves 6.

Note: Without bacon, this soup has a spa-like leanness.

Approximate nutritional analysis per serving w/ bacon:
Calories 82, Protein 5 g, Carbohydrates 10 g, Fat 3 g, Saturated Fat 1 g,
32% of Calories from Fat, Cholesterol 5 mg, Sodium 293 mg

Approximate nutritional analysis per serving w/o bacon:
Calories 58, Protein 4 g, Carbohydrates 10 g, Fat <1 g, Saturated Fat <1 g,
14% of Calories from Fat, Cholesterol 2 mg, Sodium 225 mg

Add remaining ingredients except cheese.

MEDITERRANEAN LENTIL SOUP

1 ½ cups (355 ml) dried lentils, rinsed, drained
1 - 1 lb (455 g) lamb shank, visible fat removed
1 - 1 lb can (455 g) tomatoes, coarsely chopped, liquid reserved
1 large onion, chopped
2 cloves garlic, minced
½ tsp (3 ml) salt
¾ tsp (4 ml) ground coriander
½ tsp (3 ml) ground cumin
½ tsp (3 ml) ground turmeric
1 dried small hot red pepper, crushed
4-5 cups (960-1200 ml) water
¼ cup (60 ml) minced fresh parsley
lemon wedges

Soak the top and the bottom of 3-quart (3 l) clay pot in water for 10 minutes; drain.

Combine lentils, lamb shank and tomatoes with reserved liquid in clay pot. Add onion, garlic, salt, spices and red pepper. Pour in 4 cups water.

Place covered clay pot in a cold oven. Set oven at 375°F (190°C). Bake, stirring once or twice, until lentils and lamb are very tender, 2½-3 hours.

Remove lamb shank from soup; cover soup and return to oven. When shank is cool enough to handle, discard bones, fat and any tough membrane; cut meat into bite-size pieces. Return meat to soup. Taste and add more salt, if needed. If soup is too thick, add up to 1 cup water. Bake covered 15 minutes. Stir in parsley.

Serve very hot with lemon wedges. Serves 6.

Approximate nutritional analysis per serving:
Calories 338, Protein 36 g, Carbohydrates 34 g, Fat 7 g, Saturated Fat 2 g,
17% of Calories from Fat, Cholesterol 67 mg, Sodium 246 mg

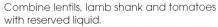

Combine lentils, lamb shank and tomatoes with reserved liquid.

HAM AND PEA SOUP

½ lb (230 g) dried peas, soaked overnight
2 tbs (30 ml) oil
1 onion, chopped
2 potatoes, peeled, diced
1 bay leaf
1 sprig rosemary
1 tsp (5 ml) dried marjoram
5 cups (1.2 l) defatted low-sodium chicken stock
1 cup (240 ml) diced, cooked lean ham
pinch crushed red pepper
pinch grated nutmeg
salt, optional
pepper, to taste
croûtons, optional

Soak the top and the bottom of 3-quart (3 l) clay pot in water for 10 minutes; drain.

Drain the peas and place them in the soaked clay pot.

Heat the oil in a saucepan. Add the onion, potatoes, bay leaf and rosemary. Cook, stirring often, for 10 minutes, until the onion is softened. Stir in the marjoram.

Tip the onion mixture into the clay pot, then pour in the stock and stir well. Add the ham. Sprinkle in a little red pepper and nutmeg but do not add salt at this stage.

Cover the clay pot and place in a cold oven. Set the oven at 400°F (205°C). Cook for 2-2½ hours or until the peas are thoroughly tender.

Taste for seasoning and sprinkle with croûtons before serving. Serves 6.

Approximate nutritional analysis per serving:
Calories 275, Protein 15 g, Carbohydrates 37 g, Fat 6 g, Saturated Fat 1 g,
21% of Calories from Fat, Cholesterol 12 mg, Sodium 366 mg

Pour in the stock and stir well.

MINESTRONE TURINESE

½ lb (230 g) cannellini beans or other white beans, soaked overnight
4 slices Canadian bacon, diced
1 large onion, chopped
2 garlic cloves, crushed
2 carrots, diced
2 potatoes, diced
4 cups (960 ml) peeled, diced tomatoes
3½ cups (840 ml) shredded cabbage
½ lb (230 g) fava beans
1 bay leaf
2 tsp (10 ml) dried marjoram
1 tbs (15 ml) salt-free tomato paste
2 qts (1.9 l) water
salt, optional
pepper, to taste
2 tbs (30 ml) chopped parsley
¼ cup (60 ml) small pasta, uncooked
freshly grated Parmesan cheese, optional

Soak the top and the bottom of 3-quart (3 l) clay pot in water for 10 minutes; drain.

Drain the cannellini beans and place them in a saucepan with cold water to cover. Bring to a boil and boil rapidly for 10 minutes, then drain the beans and place them in the soaked clay pot. Add the bacon, onion, garlic, carrots, potatoes, tomatoes, cabbage and fava beans. Mix all these ingredients together, then add the bay leaf, marjoram and tomato paste.

Pour in 2 quarts water. Cover the clay pot and place in a cold oven. Set the oven at 400°F (205°C). Cook for 1½ hours. Stir in plenty of seasoning, the parsley and pasta and cook, covered, for another 30 minutes, or until the pasta is tender.

Taste for seasoning before serving with Parmesan cheese. Serves 6.

Approximate nutritional analysis per serving:
Calories 404, Protein 26 g, Carbohydrates 72 g, Fat 3 g, Saturated Fat < 1 g,
7% of Calories from Fat, Cholesterol 10 mg, Sodium 318 mg

Peel and dice the tomatoes.

NEW ENGLAND SEAFOOD CHOWDER

1 ½ lb (680 g) mixed fish fillets and shrimp, diced
½ cup (120 ml) clam broth
1 clove garlic, crushed
3 slices Canadian bacon, chopped
1-2 tsp (5-10 ml) vegetable oil
2 large onions, chopped
½ cup (120 ml) finely chopped fresh parsley
2 medium potatoes, peeled and diced
½ cup (120 ml) water
2 medium tomatoes, chopped
½ cup (120 ml) fresh spinach, chopped
1 tsp (5ml) fresh ginger, grated
1 qt (960 ml) skim milk
2 tbs (30 ml) all-purpose flour
2 tbs (30 ml) reduced-fat margarine
salt, optional and freshly ground pepper, to taste
dash Tabasco sauce and juice of 1 lemon, for garnish

Soak the top and the bottom of 3-quart (3 l) clay pot in water for 10 minutes; drain.

Place the fish fillets, shrimp and clam broth into the presoaked clay pot. Add the Canadian bacon to the clay pot.

Heat oil in nonstick skillet, add the chopped onion and cook to golden brown. Add parsley and garlic, stir for a few minutes, then put the mixture in the clay pot.

In a saucepan, simmer the diced potatoes in ½ cup water with salt and pepper until just tender, then add potatoes, tomatoes, spinach, ginger and cooking liquid to the clay pot. Add the milk. Knead margarine and flour into a ball and add to the clay pot, with salt and pepper to taste. Cover the clay pot and place in a cold oven. Set the oven at 450°F (230°C). Cook for 40 minutes. Remove clay pot from oven and add Tabasco and lemon juice. Serves 4 as a soup course or 2 as a main course.

Approximate nutritional analysis per ¼ yield serving:
Calories 403, Protein 35 g, Carbohydrates 44 g, Fat 9 g, Saturated Fat 2 g,
21% of Calories from Fat, Cholesterol 64 mg, Sodium 735 mg

Ingredients for New England Seafood Chowder.

QUICK BASQUE FISHERMAN'S SOUP

1 medium onion, sliced
1 clove garlic, minced
1 small red or green pepper, finely chopped
1 rib celery, finely chopped
1 lb (455 g) fish fillets, such as halibut, thawed if frozen,
    cut into bite-size pieces
1 10-oz can (300 g) small whole clams, undrained
¼ lb (115 g) shelled, cooked, small deveined shrimp
½ tsp (3 ml) Italian herb seasoning
    or ⅛ tsp (.5 ml) each dried oregano and basil
pinch cayenne pepper
3 tbs (45 ml) salt-free tomato paste
1 14-oz can (420 ml) tomato purée
1 cup (240 ml) warm water
½ cup (120 ml) dry white wine
2 tbs (30 ml) minced fresh parsley

Soak top and bottom of 3-quart (3 l) clay pot in water about 10 minutes; drain. Line bottom and side of clay pot with parchment paper.

    Combine onion, garlic, red pepper and celery in clay pot. Top with fish, clams with liquid and shrimp. Sprinkle with herb seasoning and cayenne. Mix tomato paste and puree in medium bowl. Stir in warm water gradually; stir in wine. Pour mixture over fish in clay pot.

    Place covered clay pot in cold oven. Set oven at 400°F (205°C). Bake, stirring once or twice, until vegetables are crisp-tender, 1¼-1½ hours.

    Stir in parsley. Serve immediately. Serves 6.

Approximate nutritional analysis per serving:
Calories 172, Protein 25 g, Carbohydrates 10 g, Fat 3 g, Saturated Fat < 1 g,
15% of Calories from Fat, Cholesterol 64 mg, Sodium 142 mg

Cut the fish into bite-size pieces.

BLACK BEAN SOUP WITH SMOKED SAUSAGE

1 lb (455 g) dried black beans, rinsed, drained
7-7½ cups (1.7-1.8 l) water
2 ribs celery with leaves, finely chopped
2 medium onions, chopped
3 cloves garlic, minced
1 dried small hot red pepper, crushed
1 tsp (5 ml) ground coriander
¼ tsp (1 ml) ground cloves
½ lb (230 g) smoked turkey sausage, cut into 1-inch (2.5 cm) pieces
12 tsp (60 ml) reduced fat-sour cream

Place beans in a large bowl, add 4 cups of water and let stand overnight. Or heat beans and 4 cups water in 4-quart (3.8 l) kettle to boiling, boil briskly 2 minutes, remove from heat. Let stand covered 1 hour. Do not drain beans.

Soak top and bottom of 3-quart (3 l) clay pot in water about 10 minutes; drain.

Combine beans and their liquid, 3 more cups water and the remaining ingredients, except sausage and sour cream, in clay pot. Place covered clay pot in cold oven. Set oven at 375°F (190°C). Bake, stirring once or twice, until beans are nearly tender, about 2½ hours. Mash beans slightly; stir in sausage and up to ½ cup more water, if soup is too thick. Bake covered until beans are very tender, about 1 hour. Taste and add more salt, if needed.

Serve with dollops of sour cream. Serves 6.

Approximate nutritional analysis per serving:
Calories 222, Protein 14 g, Carbohydrates 27 g, Fat 7 g, Saturated Fat 3 g,
28% of Calories from Fat, Cholesterol 29 mg, Sodium 316 mg

Stir in sausage.

OLD-FASHIONED HAM AND BEAN SOUP

1 lb (455 g) dried Great Northern beans, rinsed, drained
8 cups (1.9 l) water
½ lb (230 g) smoked lean ham, diced
1 rib celery with leaves, finely chopped
1 large onion, chopped
¼ cup (60 ml) minced fresh parsley
½ tsp (3 ml) dried marjoram leaves
pinch ground cloves
1 bay leaf
salt, optional
white pepper, to taste

Place beans in large bowl, add 4 cups of water and let stand overnight. Or heat beans and 4 cups water in 4-quart (1.9 l) kettle to boiling, boil briskly 2 minutes, remove from heat. Let stand covered 1 hour. Do not drain beans.

Soak top and bottom of 3-quart (3 l) clay pot in water about 10 minutes; drain.

Combine beans and their liquid, 2 more cups of water and remaining ingredients, except salt and pepper, in clay pot. Place covered clay pot in cold oven. Set oven at 375°F (190°C). Bake, stirring once or twice, until beans are very tender, 3-3½ hours.

Mash beans slightly; stir in remaining 2 cups water. Cover soup and return to oven. Remove bay leaf. Taste and add salt and pepper, if needed. Bake covered 30 minutes.

Serve very hot. Serves 6.

Note: To lower sodium content use a low-salt or no-salt ham in recipe.

Approximate nutritional analysis per serving:
Calories 332, Protein 25 g, Carbohydrates 52 g, Fat 3 g, Saturated Fat < 1 g,
8 % of Calories from Fat, Cholesterol 20 mg, Sodium 593 mg

Add the diced ham to the pot.

FISH AND SEAFOOD

SAN FRANCISCO CLAMBAKE

2 dozen clams, in the shell
1 dozen large shrimp, in the shell
1 dozen large scallops
1 large onion, sliced thin
juice of 1 lemon
4 small green tomatoes, ground
¼ cup (60 ml) dry white wine
2 cloves garlic, crushed
2 tbs (30 ml) chopped fresh parsley
¼ tsp (1 ml) finely chopped fresh oregano
or pinch of dried oregano
pinch of dried basil
2 tbs (30 ml) olive oil
1 green pepper, sliced

Soak the top and the bottom of 3-quart (3 l) clay pot in water for 10 minutes; drain.

Wash all the shellfish in cold running water.

Line the bottom of the presoaked clay pot with the sliced onion, then add the clams. Top with the shrimp and scallops, then squeeze the lemon juice over. Add the remaining ingredients. Cover the pot and place in a cold oven. Set the oven at 450°F (230°C). Cook for 40 minutes.

When done, drain the liquid into small soup cups, do not thicken, and serve as a soup or clam broth.

Serve the shellfish with saffron rice cooked with pine nuts and pimientos. Serves 4.

Approximate nutritional analysis per serving:
Calories 276, Protein 32 g, Carbohydrates 16 g, Fat 9 g, Saturated Fat 1 g,
29% of Calories from Fat, Cholesterol 89 mg, Sodium 254 mg

Chop the herbs finely.

SPRINGTIME HALIBUT

2 lbs (910 g) small new potatoes
4 small carrots, thinly sliced
4 small zucchini, trimmed and thinly sliced
6 scallions, chopped
salt, optional
pepper, to taste
grated rind and juice of 1 lime
1 ½ lbs (685 g) halibut fillet, cut into 4 portions
1 tbs (15 ml) chopped tarragon
2 tbs (30 ml) melted butter, optional
1 ½ cups (355 ml) shelled fresh peas

Soak the top and the bottom of 3-quart (3 l) clay pot in water for 10 minutes; drain.

Cook the potatoes in boiling water for 8-10 minutes, until almost tender. Drain and place in the soaked clay pot. Blanch the carrots for 2 minutes, then add them to the potatoes. Add the zucchini, scallions, seasoning and lime rind to the vegetables in the clay pot. Mix well. Arrange the halibut on top of the vegetables, add salt and pepper to taste, then sprinkle with tarragon, lime juice and melted butter.

Cover the pot and place in the cold oven. Set the oven at 425°F (220°C). Cook for 30 minutes.

Blanch the peas in boiling water for 5 minutes, drain; add to the clay pot, carefully arranging them between the halibut portions. Cook for another 5-10 minutes or until the halibut is cooked and the vegetables are tender. Serves 4.

Approximate nutritional analysis per serving w/o melted butter:
Calories 490, Protein 45 g, Carbohydrates 68 g, Fat 5 g, Saturated Fat < 1 g,
8 % of Calories from Fat, Cholesterol 54 mg, Sodium 213 mg

Approximate nutritional analysis per serving w/ ½ tbs melted butter:
Calories 541, Protein 45 g, Carbohydrates 68 g, Fat 10 g, Saturated Fat 4 g,
17% of Calories from Fat, Cholesterol 70 mg, Sodium 214 mg

Thinly slice the vegetables.

CHINESE STEAMED FISH WITH BLACK BEANS

2 tbs (30 ml) fermented black beans*
1 large clove garlic, minced
3 thin slices peeled fresh ginger root, finely chopped
**   or ¼ tsp (1 ml) ground ginger**
¼ cup (60 ml) low-sodium soy sauce
1 tbs (15 ml) sugar
2 lbs (910 g) halibut or sea bass steaks or fillets
1 green onion with top, thinly sliced

Soak top and bottom of 3-quart (3 l) clay pot in water about 10 minutes; drain. Line bottom and sides of cooker with nonstick baking parchment or use a glazed fish baker.

Rinse and drain black beans; crush in a small bowl. Stir in garlic and ginger root to make paste. Stir in soy sauce and sugar. Wipe fish with damp paper towels. Place fish in single layer in clay pot. Spoon bean mixture over fish.

Place covered clay pot in cold oven. Set oven at 450°F (230°C). Bake until fish easily flakes with fork, about 30 minutes.

Remove fish carefully with a slotted spatula to warm serving platter; spoon on some of the cooking liquid. Sprinkle with green onions. Serves 6.

*Note: Fermented black beans are available in oriental markets. There is no substitute. Not included in the nutritional analysis due to unavailability of nutrient data.

Approximate nutritional analysis per serving:
Calories 195, Protein 32 g, Carbohydrates 1 g, Fat 6 g, Saturated Fat < 1 g.
28% of Calories from Fat, Cholesterol 48 mg, Sodium 342 mg

Crush the black beans in a small bowl.

CIOPPINO

1 large onion, finely chopped
1 green pepper, chopped
 2 cloves garlic, minced
⅓ cup (80 ml) minced fresh parsley
1 15-oz can (450 ml) salt-free tomato purée
1 8-oz can (240 ml) salt-free tomato sauce
1 cup (240 ml) water
1 cup (240 ml) dry red wine
salt, optional
pinch white pepper
¼ tsp (1 ml) dried thyme leaves
pinch dried rosemary leaves
2 1½-lb (685 g) each medium Dungeness crabs,
     cooked, cleaned, cracked
2 rock cod fillets (about ¾ lb [340 g] total),
     cut into 1½-inch (4 cm) pieces
1 lb (455 g) raw shrimp, shelled, deveined
1 dozen fresh clams in shells, scrubbed

Soak top and bottom of 4¾-quart (4.6 l) clay pot in water about 10 minutes; drain. Line bottom and sides of clay pot with nonstick baking parchment.

Combine onion, green pepper, garlic, parsley, tomato purée, tomato sauce, water, wine, optional salt, pepper, thyme and rosemary in clay pot.

Place covered clay pot in cold oven. Set oven at 425°F (220°C). Bake, stirring once or twice, until sauce is thick, about 1 hour. Stir in crab, fish fillets, shrimp and clams. Bake covered, until crab is hot, shrimp are pink and clam shells open (discard any clams that do not open), for about 45 minutes.

Serve seafood in large soup bowls; spoon sauce over seafood. Serves 6.

Approximate nutritional analysis per serving:
Calories 452, Protein 75 g, Carbohydrates 18 g, Fat 6 g, Saturated Fat <1 g,
12% of Calories from Fat, Cholesterol 297 mg, Sodium 821 mg
(*Note: crab is very high in sodium)

Fresh seafood
is a must
for Cioppino.

RED SNAPPER VERACRUZ

2 medium onions, thinly sliced, separated into rings
1 green pepper, cut into thin strips
2 cloves garlic, minced
1 1-lb can (455 g) no-salt-added tomatoes, chopped, liquid reserved
12 pimento-stuffed olives, sliced
1 tbs (15 ml) drained capers
2 tbs (30 ml) salt-free tomato paste
2 tbs (30 ml) chopped fresh coriander leaves
2 tsp (10 ml) grated orange rind
salt, to taste
½ tsp (3 ml) dried oregano leaves
½ tsp (3 ml) ground cumin
1 bay leaf
1 dried small red chili pepper, crushed
2 lbs (910 g) red snapper fillets
salt and pepper, to taste
coriander sprigs, if desired

Soak top and bottom of 3-quart (3 l) clay pot in water about 10 minutes; drain. Line bottom and sides of cooker with nonstick baking parchment.

Combine the onions, green pepper, garlic, tomatoes, olives, capers, tomato paste, coriander, orange rind, salt to taste, oregano, cumin, bay leaf and dried chili pepper; add to clay pot. Place covered clay pot in a cold oven. Set oven at 450°F (230°C). Bake, stirring once or twice, until sauce is flavorful and thick, about 2 hours.

Wipe fillets with damp paper towels. Sprinkle both sides lightly with salt, if desired, and pepper. Remove and reserve about half the sauce from clay pot; discard bay leaf. Place fish fillets, slightly overlapping, in remaining sauce in clay pot. Cover with reserved sauce. Bake covered until fish is white and firm, about 20 minutes. Garnish with coriander sprigs. Serves 6.

Approximate nutritional analysis per serving:
Calories 216, Protein 33 g, Carbohydrates 13 g, Fat 3 g, Saturated Fat 1 g,
14% of Calories from Fat, Cholesterol 56 mg, Sodium 412 mg

Place fish fillets, slightly overlapping, in remaining sauce in clay pot

SEA BASS ITALIANO

1 medium onion, sliced thin
1 green pepper, sliced
4 medium mushrooms, sliced thin
4 slices sea bass (2½ lbs [1.1 kg])
salt, optional
1 clove garlic, minced
½ tsp (3 ml) dried oregano
½ tsp (3 ml) dried marjoram
½ cup (120 ml) salt-free tomato sauce
½ cup (120 ml) fish stock
1½ tsp (8 ml) arrowroot, approximately

Soak the top and the bottom of 3-quart (3 l) clay pot in water for 10 minutes; drain.

Place the onion, green pepper and mushrooms in the bottom of the presoaked clay pot; lay slices of bass on top. Combine the optional salt, garlic, herbs, tomato sauce and fish stock and pour over the fish.

Cover the clay pot and place it in a cold oven. Set the oven at 450°F (230°C). Cook for 45 minutes. When done, remove the pot from the oven and pour off the sauce into a saucepan. Heat and thicken with the arrowroot, pour sauce over each portion. Serves 4.

Approximate nutritional analysis per serving:
Calories 311, Protein 55 g, Carbohydrates 12 g, Fat 4 g, Saturated Fat <1 g,
11% of Calories from Fat, Cholesterol 136 mg, Sodium 240 mg

Place onion, green pepper and mushrooms in bottom of the presoaked clay pot; lay slices of bass on top.

ROCK COD IN A HURRY

2 lbs (910 g) rock cod
1 lemon
2 tbs (30 ml) melted butter
¼ cup (60 ml) white wine
1 onion, sliced thin
6 medium mushrooms, sliced thin
salt, optional
freshly ground pepper, to taste
capers, optional, to taste
1 tsp (5 ml) arrowroot, approximately

Wash the fish in cold running water, then squeeze the juice of the lemon over the fish and let stand while the pot is soaking. Set the juiced lemon aside.

Soak the top and the bottom of 3-quart (3 l) clay pot in water for 10 minutes; drain.

When ready to cook, brush the fish with the melted butter. Slice the reserved juiced lemon and place it both inside and outside of the fish. Place the fish in the pot; add white wine, onion, mushrooms, optional salt and pepper.

Cover the clay pot and put it in a cold oven. Set the oven at 450°F (230°C). Cook for 45 minutes.

Five minutes before cooking time is up, remove the clay pot from the oven and pour off liquid into a saucepan, return the uncovered clay pot to the oven for the last 5 minutes of cooking time to brown the fish.

Meanwhile, add a dash of white wine and the arrowroot to the liquid and stir until thickened. Pour sauce over fish. Add capers, if desired, to taste. Serves 4.

Approximate nutritional analysis per serving:
Calories 280, Protein 42 g, Carbohydrates 9 g, Fat 8 g, Saturated Fat 4 g,
25% of Calories from Fat, Cholesterol 113 mg, Sodium 126 mg

Squeeze the juice of the lemon over the fish.

SAUSALITO RED SNAPPER

1 small clove garlic, crushed
2 tbs (30 ml) chopped fresh parsley
½ small onion, minced
2 tbs (30 ml) olive oil
4 red snapper fillets
cayenne pepper, to taste
¼ cup (60 ml) dry white wine
6 capers
1 tsp (5 ml) minced fresh tarragon
    or ½ tsp (3 ml) dried tarragon
1 tsp (5 ml) low-sodium Worcestershire sauce
dash Tabasco sauce
juice of ½ lemon
1 tsp (5 ml) arrowroot, approximately

Soak the top and the bottom of 3-quart (3 l) clay pot in water for 10 minutes; drain.

Sauté the garlic, parsley and onion in the olive oil until golden brown, then paint the mixture on both sides of each snapper slice, adding a dash of cayenne to each side.

Combine the white wine, capers, tarragon, Worcestershire sauce, Tabasco, and lemon juice in a saucepan. Bring to a boil, stir, crushing the tarragon and capers.

Place the fish in the presoaked clay pot and cover with the sauce. Cover the clay pot and place it in a cold oven. Set the oven at 450°F (230 °C). Cook for 30 minutes.

Remove the clay pot from the oven and pour off the liquid into a saucepan. Heat the liquid and add the arrowroot to thicken, then pour the sauce back into the clay pot. Return the pot to the oven, without the lid, for 5 minutes to brown the fish. Serves 4.

Approximate nutritional analysis per serving:
Calories 249, Protein 47 g, Carbohydrates 4 g, Fat 3 g, Saturated Fat <1 g,
12% of Calories from Fat, Cholesterol 84 mg, Sodium 180 mg

Paint the mixture on both sides of each snapper slice.

CARDAMOM COD STEAKS

4 cod steaks
4 cardamom pods
2 small zucchini, trimmed and grated
1 cup (240 ml) fresh bread crumbs
4 tbs (60 ml) snipped chives
2 tbs (30 ml) low-fat plain yogurt
salt, optional
pepper, to taste
2 tbs (30 ml) melted butter
lemon slices to garnish

Soak the top and the bottom of 3-quart (3 l) clay pot in water for 10 minutes; drain.

Cut the central bone out of the cod steaks, then lay them in the presoaked clay pot. Split open each cardamom pod and carefully transfer the tiny black seeds to a mortar. Grind them to a powder using a pestle, then sprinkle the powder over the cod steaks. Mix the zucchini, bread crumbs and chives in a bowl. Stir in the yogurt and seasoning, then spread equal amounts of stuffing on each cod steak. Brush the melted butter over the fish.

Cover the clay pot and place it in a cold oven. Set the oven at 425°F (220°C). Cook for 35-40 minutes or until the fish is cooked and the top of the stuffing is lightly browned.

Serve at once, garnished with halved lemon slices, with the cooking juices poured over. Serves 4.

Approximate nutritional analysis per serving:
Calories 344, Protein 44 g, Carbohydrates 20 g, Fat 9 g, Saturated Fat 4 g,
23% of Calories from Fat, Cholesterol 115 mg, Sodium 313 mg

Spread equal amounts of stuffing on each cod steak.

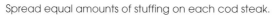

MARINATED TUNA WITH BEANS

1 ½ lbs (685 g) tuna steak
salt, optional
pepper, to taste
4 sprigs thyme
4 bay leaves
6 tbs (90 ml) snipped chives
grated rind and juice of 1 lime
4 tbs (60 ml) olive oil
4 tbs (60 ml) dry sherry
1 lb (455 g) green beans, trimmed
½ red onion, thinly sliced
lime wedges, to garnish

Soak the top and the bottom of 3-quart (3 l) clay pot in water for 10 minutes; drain.

Place the tuna in a dish. Season well, then top with the thyme, bay leaves and chives. Mix the lime rind and juice, olive oil and sherry in a bowl, then pour it over the fish. Cover and leave to marinate for at least 3 hours.

Transfer to the soaked clay pot. Cover the pot and place in a cold oven. Set the oven at 425°F (220°C). Cook for 25 minutes.

Meanwhile, add the beans to a saucepan of boiling and lightly salted water. Bring back to a boil and cook for 2 minutes. Drain. Add the beans to the pot and cook, covered, for another 10-15 minutes or until the fish is cooked through.

Baste tuna with the juices and divide between serving plates, with the beans. Add the sliced raw onion and garnish with lime wedges. Serves 4.

Approximate nutritional analysis per serving:
Calories 328, Protein 42 g, Carbohydrates 11 g, Fat 12 g, Saturated Fat g,
33% of Calories from Fat, Cholesterol 65 mg, Sodium 75 mg

Add the beans to the pot and cook.

SPICY FISH FILLETS

1 lb (455 g) spinach, trimmed
1 tbs (15 ml) butter or margarine
1 tbs (15 ml) vegetable oil
2 garlic cloves, minced
3 tbs (45 ml) grated fresh ginger root
1 tbs (15 ml) cumin seeds
4 cardamom pods
1 tbs (15 ml) ground coriander
1 tsp (5 ml) ground turmeric
2 tbs (30 ml) low-fat plain yogurt
salt and pepper, to taste
½ lb (230 g) peeled shrimp
2 lbs (910 g) white fish fillets, such as sole, skinned
4 tomatoes, peeled and chopped
1 tbs (15 ml) chopped cilantro
lemon wedges, to garnish

Soak the top and the bottom of 3-quart (3 l) clay pot in water for 10 minutes; drain.

Wash the spinach, then put the wet leaves in a large saucepan. Cover and cook over high heat, shaking the pan often, for about 5 minutes or until the leaves have shrunk. Drain well, then place the spinach in the soaked clay pot.

Melt the butter or margarine in a nonstick pan with the oil. Add the garlic and ginger root and cook for 3 minutes, stirring, then add the cumin, cardamom pods, coriander and turmeric and cook for another 2 minutes. Remove from the heat and stir in the yogurt and seasoning to taste. Spread the shrimp out over the spinach. Arrange the fish fillets over the top, then spoon the spice mixture over. Cover the clay pot and place in a cold oven. Set the oven at 425°F (220°C). Cook for 40 minutes or until the fish is just firm.

Top with the tomatoes and sprinkle with the chopped cilantro, then serve garnished with lemon wedges. Basmati rice or nan bread are ideal accompaniments. Serves 4.

Approximate nutritional analysis per serving:
Calories 394, Protein 60 g, Carbohydrates 14 g, Fat 11 g, Saturated Fat 3 g,
25% of Calories from Fat, Cholesterol 203 mg, Sodium 379 mg

Arrange the fish filets over the top.

MIXED SEAFOOD WITH FENNEL AND TOMATO

2-3 tbs (30-45 ml) olive oil
1 onion, sliced
2 bulbs fennel, sliced
salt, optional
pepper, to taste
1 28-oz can (840 g) chopped tomatoes
½ lb (230 g) peeled, cooked shrimp
½ lb (230 g) shelled, cooked mussels
8 shelled, raw scallops
1 lb (455 g) white fish fillets, skinned, cut in chunks
8 black olives, pitted, sliced
4 large sprigs basil, shredded

Soak the top and the bottom of 3-quart (3 l) clay pot in water for 10 minutes; drain.

Heat the oil in a nonstick saucepan. Add the onion and fennel. Season to taste and cook, stirring often, for 20 minutes, or until the onion and fennel are softened. Stir in the tomatoes and bring to a boil. Simmer for 3 minutes, then turn the mixture into the presoaked clay pot.

Mix the shrimp, mussels and scallops into the tomato and fennel mixture in the clay pot. Add the white fish, distributing the chunks on the surface of the tomato mixture.

Cover the clay pot and place in a cold oven. Set the oven at 425°F (220°C). Cook for 35 minutes or until the fish is cooked. Taste for seasoning, then mix the fish gently into the sauce, adding the olives and basil.

Serve at once, with rice, pasta or chunks of crusty bread. Serves 4.

Approximate nutritional analysis per serving:
Calories 390, Protein 51 g, Carbohydrates 18 g, Fat 12 g, Saturated Fat 2 g,
29% of Calories from Fat, Cholesterol 175 mg, Sodium 575 mg

Fennel and tomatoes make this dish special.

POULTRY

LOUISIANA JAMBALAYA

1 large onion, chopped
1 green bell pepper, diced
1 garlic clove, crushed
¼-½ tsp (1-3 ml) chili powder
1 tsp (5 ml) dried oregano
1 bay leaf
1½ cups (355 ml) long-grain rice
½ lb (230 g) smoked turkey sausage
4 tomatoes, peeled, diced
3¾ cups (900 ml) defatted low-sodium chicken stock
salt, optional
pepper, to taste
2 tbs (30 ml) chopped parsley
16 large shrimp

Soak the top and the bottom of 3-quart (3 l) clay pot in water for 10 minutes; drain.

Place the onion, green pepper, garlic, chili powder, oregano and bay leaf in the presoaked clay pot. Add the rice, turkey sausage and tomatoes; mix well, then pour in the stock. Sprinkle in a little seasoning to taste.

Cover the clay pot and place in a cold oven. Set oven at 425°F (220°C). Cook for 30 minutes. Stir the mixture, then cook, covered, for another 30 minutes.

Sprinkle the parsley over the rice, then arrange the shrimp on top. Cook, covered, for another 15 minutes, or until the shrimp are pink and heated through.

Serve with a crisp green salad and crusty bread. Serves 4.

Approximate nutritional analysis per serving:
Calories 455, Protein 21 g, Carbohydrates 68 g, Fat 9 g, Saturated Fat 1 g,
19% of Calories from Fat, Cholesterol 81 mg, Sodium 490 mg

Dice the vegetables.

BAKER'S CHICKEN

1 lemon, sliced
2 bay leaves
2 lbs (910 g) potatoes, sliced
1 large onion, thinly sliced
4 tbs (60 ml) chopped tarragon
salt, optional
pepper, to taste
2 tbs (30 ml) olive oil or melted butter
4 chicken quarters, skin removed

Soak the top and the bottom of 3-quart (3 l) clay pot in water for 10 minutes; drain.
   Lay half the lemon slices in the bottom of the presoaked clay pot. Add the bay leaves, then layer the potatoes and onion on top. Sprinkle half the tarragon and season with salt and pepper to taste. Sprinkle half the olive oil over the potatoes and onions and arrange the chicken quarters on top. Season them and sprinkle with the remaining tarragon. Pour the rest of the olive oil over the chicken quarters, then tuck the remaining lemon slices around them.
   Cover the clay pot and place in a cold oven. Set the oven at 425°F (220°C). Cook for 40 minutes. Uncover the clay pot and cook for another 15-20 minutes, or until the chicken quarters are cooked through, crisp and golden. The vegetables should be tender. Serve the chicken with the potatoes and onions; discard the lemon slices, which are included for flavor, or use them as a garnish. Serve with seasonal vegetables. Serves 4.

Approximate nutritional analysis per serving:
Calories 416, Protein 31 g, Carbohydrates 50 g, Fat 10 g, Saturated Fat 2 g,
22% of Calories from Fat, Cholesterol 87 mg, Sodium 108 mg

Lay half the lemon slices in the bottom of the clay pot.

CHINESE BEGGAR'S CHICKEN

4 chicken drumsticks or thighs
2 chicken breasts on the bone, skin removed
1 tsp (5 ml) sesame oil
1 tbs (15 ml) dry sherry
¼ tsp (1 ml) five-spice powder
¼ tsp (1 ml) ground white pepper
1 garlic clove, crushed
1 tsp (5 ml) grated fresh ginger root
3 tbs (45 ml) low-sodium soy sauce
8 scallions, to garnish
1 tbs (15 ml) sesame seeds, lightly toasted

Make two or three slits into the meat on each chicken piece, then place them in a dish. Mix together the oil, sherry, five-spice powder, pepper, garlic, ginger root and soy sauce, then brush the mixture over the chicken pieces, using all the marinade. Cover and chill for at least 5 hours or preferably overnight. Turn several times.

Soak the top and the bottom of 3-quart (3 l) clay pot in water for 10 minutes; drain.

Meanwhile trim the scallions and cut the green part into fine strips, all attached at the root end. Place in iced water for at least 30 minutes so that the strips curl.

Transfer the chicken to the soaked clay pot with all the marinating juices. Cover the clay pot and place in a cold oven. Set the oven at 475°F (246°C). Cook for 35 minutes. Baste the chicken well with the cooking juices and sprinkle with the sesame seeds. Cook, uncovered, for another 15 minutes.

Serve piping hot with cooked rice, garnished with the scallion curls. Serves 4.

Approximate nutritional analysis per serving:
Calories 168, Protein 27 g, Carbohydrates 1 g, Fat 5 g, Saturated Fat 1 g,
29% of Calories from Fat, Cholesterol 82 mg, Sodium 386 mg

Brush the mixture over the chicken pieces.

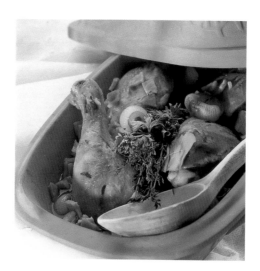

COQ AU VIN

4 chicken quarters, skinned, wing removed from breast
1 garlic clove, crushed
1 bouquet garni, an herb bundle containing a few sprigs of parsley,
thyme and a bay leaf
salt and pepper, to taste
4 cups (960 ml) red wine
2 tbs (30 ml) olive oil
¾ lb (340 g) pearl onions, halved if large
2 oz (60 g) Canadian bacon, diced
¾ lb (340 g) button mushrooms
1 tbs (15 ml) cornstarch
2 tbs (30 ml) water
4 tbs (60 ml) chopped parsley
croûtons, to garnish

Place the chicken quarters in a bowl. Whisk together the garlic, bouquet garni, salt, pepper and wine and pour over the chicken. Cover and chill for 24 hours.

Soak the top and bottom of 3-quart (3 l) clay pot in water for 10 minutes; drain.

Heat the oil in a nonstick skillet. Brown onions in 1 tablespoon oil. Remove; set aside. Lift the chicken from the bowl, pat dry, then brown the portions in second tablespoon oil all over. Place in the presoaked clay pot. Add onions, marinade and Canadian bacon.

Cover the pot and place in a cold oven. Set the oven at 425°F (220°C). Cook for 45 minutes. Add the mushrooms to the pot and cook for another 45 minutes, until the chicken is tender and cooked.

Meanwhile, combine cornstarch and water. Pour the cooking sauce into a saucepan and transfer the chicken to warmed plates. Boil the sauce and add half the cornstarch mixture. Add additional cornstarch and water to reach desired thickness. Boil, whisking for 3 minutes. Ladle the sauce over the chicken, sprinkle generously with parsley and garnish with croûtons. Serves 4.

Approximate nutritional analysis per serving:
Calories 373, Protein 33 g, Carbohydrates 16 g, Fat 11 g, Saturated Fat 2 g,
28% of Calories from Fat, Cholesterol 94 mg, Sodium 305 mg

Dice the Canadian bacon finely.

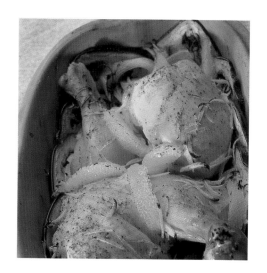

TURKISH CHICKEN

2 large eggplants, sliced
salt, optional
pepper, to taste
1 tbs (15 ml) canola or vegetable oil
1 onion, sliced
1 tbs (15 ml) ground coriander
4 chicken quarters, wing and skin removed
8 thyme sprigs
5 oranges
grated nutmeg

Place the eggplant slices in a strainer, sprinkling each layer with salt, if desired. Set aside over a bowl for 30 minutes.*

Soak the top and the bottom of 3-quart (3 l) clay pot in water for 10 minutes; drain.

Rinse and pat dry the eggplant, then place in the presoaked clay pot.

Heat oil in a nonstick skillet, add the onion and cook for 3 minutes. Sprinkle the coriander over the eggplant, then spread the onion slices on top and pour the cooking juices over. Place the chicken quarters in the pot, tucking a thyme sprig under each one. Grate the rind and squeeze the juice from 1 orange. Sprinkle nutmeg and seasoning over the chicken quarters.

Cover the clay pot and place in a cold oven. Set the oven at 425°F (220°C). Cook for 40 minutes. Cut all the peel and pith from the remaining oranges, then slice them, discarding the seeds. Arrange around the chicken. Cook, covered, for another 15-20 minutes.

Serve garnished with the remaining thyme sprigs. Serves 4.

*Note: For those whose sodium intake is limited this step can be omitted without significant impact to the recipe.

Approximate nutritional analysis per serving:
Calories 298, Protein 30 g, Carbohydrates 31 g, Fat 7 g, Saturated Fat 1 g,
20% of Calories from Fat, Cholesterol 87 mg, Sodium 103 mg

Sprinkle nutmeg and seasoning over the chicken.

GINGERED ROAST CHICKEN WITH NECTARINES

1 3½-lb (1.6 kg) whole frying chicken
2 large nectarines unpeeled, cut into wedges, pitted
2 tbs (30 ml) brown sugar
½ tsp (3 ml) ground ginger
¼ tsp (1 ml) nutmeg
1 tbs (15 ml) butter

Soak top and bottom of 2-quart (1.9 l) clay pot in water about 10 minutes; drain.

Rinse chicken and pat dry, reserving neck and giblets for other use. Place chicken, breast side up, in clay pot. Surround with nectarines. Mix brown sugar, ginger and nutmeg; sprinkle over chicken and fruit. Dot chicken and fruit with butter.

Place covered clay pot in cold oven. Set oven at 475°F (246°C). Bake 1 hour. Remove cover; bake until chicken is crisp and brown, 5-10 minutes.

Carve chicken; spoon fruit and cooking juices over chicken. Serves 4.

Note: This chicken is delicious whole roasted, but a considerable number of calories and fat can be pared by substituting skinless chicken parts. Further reductions can be enjoyed by using skinless breasts only.

Approximate nutritional analysis per serving (whole chicken w/ skin):
Calories 842, Protein 115 g, Carbohydrates 16 g, Fat 32 g, Saturated Fat 10 g,
36% of Calories from Fat, Cholesterol 359 mg, Sodium 343 mg

Approximate nutritional analysis per serving (chicken pieces w/o skin):
Calories 230, Protein 27 g, Carbohydrates 16 g, Fat 6 g, Saturated Fat 2 g,
24% of Calories from Fat, Cholesterol 95 mg, Sodium 98 mg

Cut the nectarines into wedges.

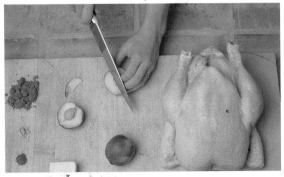

TANDOORI CHICKEN

2 2½-lb (910-1138 g each) whole small frying chickens
2 tbs (30 ml) lime or lemon juice
1 tsp (5 ml) salt
⅔ cup (160 ml) low-fat plain yogurt
2 cloves garlic, minced
2 tsp (10 ml) pared grated fresh ginger root or ½ tsp (3 ml) ground ginger
1 tsp (5 ml) ground cumin
1 tsp (5 ml) ground coriander
¼ tsp (1 ml) cayenne pepper
¼ tsp (1 ml) red food coloring, optional
pinch powdered saffron or saffron threads
green onions
lime or lemon wedges
fresh coriander sprigs
radishes

One or two days before cooking, remove and discard skin from each chicken; reserve necks and giblets for other use. Pierce breasts, thighs and legs in several places with fork. Place chickens in shallow glass baking dish; spoon on lime juice slowly. Sprinkle evenly with salt.

Mix yogurt, garlic, ginger, cumin, coriander, cayenne, food coloring, if desired, and saffron. Spread yogurt mixture evenly over chicken. Cover lightly. Refrigerate 1-2 days.

Soak top and bottom of 3-4¾-quart (3-4.6 l) clay pot in water for 10 minutes; drain. Place chickens, breast sides up, in clay pot; spoon any remaining marinade over chicken. Place covered clay pot in a cold oven. Set oven at 475°F (246°C). Bake until chicken is tender and juices run clear when thigh is pierced, about 1 hour. Remove cover; bake until coating is crusty and brown, 5-10 minutes.

Cut chickens in half; garnish with green onions, lime wedges, coriander sprigs and radishes. Serve with basmati rice. Serves 8.

Approximate nutritional analysis per serving:
Calories 273, Protein 50 g, Carbohydrates 2 g, Fat 6 g, Saturated Fat 2 g,
20% of Calories from Fat, Cholesterol 158 mg, Sodium 452 mg

Remove and discard skin from each chicken.

BAKED CHICKEN WITH ARTICHOKES

¼ lb (115 g) mushrooms, thinly sliced
1 small onion, finely chopped
1 clove garlic, finely chopped
3 lbs (1.4 kg) chicken (1½ lbs [685 g] breasts, skin removed,
    plus 1½ lbs [685 g] thighs and drumsticks, skin removed)
2 tbs (30 ml) flour
salt, optional
½ tsp (3 ml) paprika
¼ tsp (1 ml) dried rosemary leaves, crumbled
pinch white pepper
½ cup (120 ml) defatted low-sodium chicken broth
¼ cup (60 ml) dry sherry
1 10-oz pkg (300 g) frozen artichoke hearts
    or 1 14-oz can (420 g) artichoke hearts, drained

Soak the top and the bottom of 3-quart (3 l) clay pot in water for 10 minutes; drain.

Place mushrooms, onion and garlic in presoaked clay pot. Coat chicken pieces with mixture of flour, optional salt, paprika, rosemary and pepper. Arrange chicken pieces, flesh side up, in even layers over vegetables. Pour in chicken broth and sherry.

Place covered clay pot in a cold oven. Set oven at 450°F (230°C). Bake just until chicken is tender, about 1 hour. Stir in artichoke hearts gently. Bake covered until artichokes are hot, 8-10 minutes more. Serves 6

Note: Adding 2 lbs (910 g) new potatoes cut in half plus another ½ cup (120 ml) stock transforms this into a hearty stew.

Approximate nutritional analysis per serving:
Calories 313, Protein 52 g, Carbohydrates 10 g, Fat 6 g, Saturated Fat 2 g,
18% of Calories from Fat, Cholesterol 156 mg, Sodium 199 mg

Thinly slice mushrooms.

CHICKEN WITH CHEDDAR AND GREEN CHILIES

3 lbs (1.4 kg) chicken breasts, skin removed
2 tbs (30 ml) flour
2 tsp (10 ml) chili powder
½ tsp (3 ml) ground cumin
1 rib celery, finely chopped
1 small onion, finely chopped
1 clove garlic, minced
1 4-oz can (120 g) diced green chili peppers
½ cup (120 ml) defatted low-sodium chicken broth,
    canned or homemade
½ cup (120 ml) reduced-fat sour cream
1 cup (240 ml) reduced-fat shredded cheddar cheese

Soak the top and the bottom of 3-quart (3 l) clay pot in water for 10 minutes; drain.

Coat chicken pieces with mixture of flour, chili powder and cumin. Combine celery, onion and garlic in presoaked clay pot. Top with chicken and green chilies. Pour in chicken broth.

Place covered clay pot in a cold oven. Set oven at 450°F (230°C). Bake, stirring once or twice, until chicken is tender and brown, about 1¼ hours. Remove chicken from clay pot. Skim and discard fat from cooking liquid in clay pot. Stir sour cream into cooking liquid until smooth. Return chicken to sauce. Sprinkle with cheese. Bake, uncovered, until cheese melts and browns, about 10 minutes. Serves 6.

Approximate nutritional analysis per serving:
Calories 357, Protein 59 g, Carbohydrates 7 g, Fat 9 g, Saturated Fat 4 g,
23% of Calories from Fat, Cholesterol 152 mg, Sodium 304 mg

Coat chicken with flour, chili powder and cumin.

CURRIED CHICKEN WITH GUINNESS

3 tbs (45 ml) flour
3 tbs (45 ml) good Indian curry powder
salt, optional
1 - 2¹/₂-3 lb (1.1-1.4 kg) frying chicken, skinned,
    cut into bite-size pieces
8 little white onions, peeled
3 cups (720 ml) cubed fresh pineapple, or unsweetened canned
1 green pepper, sliced
¹/₃ cup (80 ml) dried currants
³/₄ cup (180 ml) Guinness stout or dark ale

Soak the top and the bottom of 3-quart (3 l) clay pot in water for 10 minutes; drain.
    Combine flour, curry powder and optional salt in paper bag, add chicken pieces and shake well. Add remaining flour mixture to the presoaked clay pot, along with all the other ingredients. Place chicken on top of vegetables.
    Place covered clay pot in a cold oven. Set oven at 480°F (249°C). Cook 70 minutes, stirring once.
    Serve over rice. Serves 4.

Approximate nutritional analysis per serving:
Calories 319, Protein 29 g, Carbohydrates 43 g, Fat 3 g, Saturated Fat <1 g,
10% of Calories from Fat, Cholesterol 87 mg, Sodium 102 mg

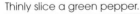
Thinly slice a green pepper.

ORANGE CHICKEN

3-4 lb (1.4-1.8 kg) chicken, skin removed
salt, optional
pepper, to taste
1 clove garlic, crushed
2 medium oranges, grated, then peeled and sliced
½ cup (120 ml) orange juice
¼ cup (60 ml) low-sodium soy sauce
1 tsp (5 ml) grated fresh ginger root
½ tsp (3 ml) allspice, ground
1 tbs (15 ml) brown sugar
arrowroot, optional

Soak the top and the bottom of 3-quart (3 l) clay pot in water for 10 minutes; drain.

Wash chicken, inside and out, under running cold water. Rub inside of chicken with salt, pepper and crushed garlic. Stuff with peeled orange slices. Place chicken in pre-soaked clay pot, breast down. Sprinkle grated orange rind over chicken. Combine orange juice, soy sauce, ginger root, allspice and brown sugar and pour over chicken.

Place covered clay pot in a cold oven. Set oven at 480°F (249°C). Cook 90 minutes. After 80 minutes, remove clay pot from oven and pour liquid into saucepan. Return the clay pot, uncovered, to oven for final 10 minutes to brown the chicken.

Meanwhile, bring sauce to a boil and thicken with arrowroot, if desired. You may want to add a bit of brown sugar to the sauce, to taste.

Serves 4.

Approximate nutritional analysis per serving:
Calories 213, Protein 28 g, Carbohydrates 16 g, Fat 3 g, Saturated Fat <1 g,
14% of Calories from Fat, Cholesterol 87 mg, Sodium 487 mg

Stuff chicken with peeled orange slices.

ISRAELI CHICKEN WITH KUMQUATS

3-4 lb (1.4-1.8 kg) frying chicken, skin removed,
**   cut into serving pieces**
salt, optional
½ cup (120 ml) orange juice
2 tbs (30 ml) lemon juice
¼ cup (60 ml) honey
4 hot chili peppers, seeded and chopped fine
8 preserved kumquats

Soak the top and the bottom of 3-quart (3 l) clay pot in water for 10 minutes; drain.

Rub chicken parts with salt, if desired, and place in presoaked clay pot. Combine orange juice, lemon juice and honey and pour over the chicken. Add the chilies.

Place the covered clay pot in a cold oven. Set oven at 480°F (249°C). Cook 25 minutes. Remove from oven, baste chicken with pot liquid and add kumquats. Return covered clay pot to oven and cook for 10 minutes. Remove clay pot from oven, baste again and return clay pot uncovered to oven for another 10 minutes to brown chicken. Serves 4.

Approximate nutritional analysis per serving:
Calories 247, Protein 27 g, Carbohydrates 21 g, Fat 3 g, Saturated Fat <1 g,
12% of Calories from Fat, Cholesterol 87 mg, Sodium 97 mg

Combine orange juice, lemon juice and honey
and pour over the chicken.

CHICKEN CARIBE

12 pieces frying chicken, skin removed
2 tbs (30 ml) flour
½ lb (230 g) smoked turkey sausage, in 1-inch slices
salt, optional
2 tbs (30 ml) olive oil
2 red torpedo onions, sliced thin
1 green pepper, sliced thin
1 sweet red pepper, sliced thin
½ cup pitted green olives
3 cloves garlic, crushed
1 mango, green as possible, sliced
1 banana, sliced thin
4 pineapple slices, cut into chunks
1 cup (240 ml) shelled green peas
2 apples, sliced
1 tsp (5 ml) black pepper
¼ tsp (1 ml) red pepper flakes
arrowroot

Soak the top and the bottom of 3-quart (3 l) clay pot in water for 10 minutes; drain.

Toss the chicken with seasoned flour to coat. Brown the chicken and sausage in a large nonstick pan with the olive oil. Place in presoaked clay pot. Add the onions, peppers, olives and garlic to the clay pot.

Cover the clay pot and place in a cold oven. Set oven at 450°F (230°C). Cook for 30 minutes. Remove clay pot from oven and pour off liquid into the frying pan. Add to the clay pot the mangos, banana, pineapple, peas, apples, black pepper and hot pepper. Return the covered clay pot to the oven. Cook an additional 30 minutes.

Meanwhile, skim or siphon off excess fat from the sauce and pour it into a saucepan. Heat the liquid in the frying pan and thicken with arrowroot. Serves 8.

Approximate nutritional analysis per serving:
Calories 491, Protein 61 g, Carbohydrates 29 g, Fat 11 g, Saturated Fat 3 g,
26% of Calories from Fat, Cholesterol 192 mg, Sodium 430 mg

Slice and dice fruits and vegetables.

GAME HENS WITH RICE AND ALMONDS

⅓ cup (80 ml) wild rice
salt, optional
⅓ cup (80 ml) long-grain rice
1 small onion, chopped
grated rind and juice of 1 orange
3 1-lb (455 g each) Cornish game hens
1 tbs (15 ml) melted butter
1 tbs (15 ml) clear honey
pinch turmeric
1½ tsp (8 ml) fresh grated ginger
1 tsp (5 ml) ground coriander
2 tbs (30 ml) slivered almonds
1 cup (240 ml) low-fat plain yogurt
2-inch (5 cm) piece cucumber, grated
1 tsp (5 ml) chopped mint

Soak the top and the bottom of 3-quart (3 l) clay pot in water for 10 minutes; drain.

Cook the wild rice in boiling salted water for 30 minutes. Drain. Simmer the long-grain rice and onion in a covered saucepan with water for 20 minutes. Mix both types of rice. Add the orange juice, grated orange rind and seasoning.

Spoon the rice into the body cavities of the Cornish game hens, then place them in the presoaked clay pot. Mix the butter, honey, turmeric, ginger and coriander. Brush the butter mixture all over the Cornish game hens and season well.

Cover the clay pot and place in a cold oven Set oven at 400°F (205°C). Cook for 45 minutes. Sprinkle the birds with the almonds. Cook, covered, for another 25-30 minutes, until the birds are golden and cooked through.

Mix together the yogurt, cucumber and mint and serve on the side with the birds. Serves 6.

Approximate nutritional analysis per serving:
Calories 658, Protein 65 g, Carbohydrates 55 g, Fat 20 g, Saturated Fat 6 g,
27% of Calories from Fat, Cholesterol 192 mg, Sodium 210 mg

Spoon the rice into the body cavities of the Cornish game hens.

FESTIVE CHICKEN

4 boneless chicken breasts, skinned
salt, optional, or to taste
pepper, to taste
½ tsp (3 ml) ground mace
1 tbs (15 ml) vegetable oil
¼ lb (115 g) pearl onions, halved
1 tbs (15 ml) butter
1 tbs (15 ml) all-purpose flour
4 tbs (60 ml) brandy
1 cup (240 ml) dry white wine
½ lb (230 g) dried apricots, halved
¼ lb (115 g) dried pitted prunes, halved
4 bay leaves
¼ lb (115 g) small button mushrooms

Soak the top and the bottom of 3-quart (3 l) clay pot in water for 10 minutes; drain.

Make two or three cuts across each chicken breast, then season well and sprinkle with mace. Heat half the oil in a nonstick skillet and brown the chicken, then place chicken in the presoaked clay pot.

Brown the onions in the remaining oil in the nonstick skillet, then transfer them to the clay pot. Wipe clean the skillet. Melt the butter in the skillet and stir in the flour. Pour in the brandy and wine, then bring to a boil, stirring. Remove from the heat and add the apricots, prunes, bay leaves and mushrooms. Stir well; pour the mixture over the chicken.

Cover the clay pot and place in a cold oven. Set the oven at 425°F (220°C). Cook for 50 minutes or until the chicken is cooked through.

Season to taste and serve. Serves 4.

Approximate nutritional analysis per serving:
Calories 379, Protein 30 g, Carbohydrates 42 g, Fat 8 g, Saturated Fat <1 g,
20% of Calories from Fat, Cholesterol 76 mg, Sodium 85 mg

Make two or three cuts across each chicken breast.

MOROCCAN TAGINE

½ tsp (3 ml) freshly ground pepper
½ tsp (3 ml) ground turmeric
1 tsp (5 ml) ground ginger
¾ tsp (4 ml) ground cinnamon
3 lbs (1.4 kg) boneless, skinless chicken breasts or lean beef,
   cut into chunks
1 large onion, chopped coarsely
1 tbs (15 ml) vegetable oil
1½ cups (355 ml) water
1 lb (455 g) pitted prunes, soaked if too dry
4 small zucchini, scrubbed and cut into 1-inch (2.5 cm) lengths
¼ cup (60 ml) chopped fresh parsley
¼ cup (60 ml) chopped fresh coriander
½ tsp (3 ml) dried oregano
½ tsp (3 ml) dried thyme
¼ cup (60 ml) honey
4 tart apples
½ cup (120 ml) slivered almonds
1 tbs (15 ml) butter

Soak the top and the bottom of 3-quart (3 l) clay pot in water for 10 minutes; drain.

In a saucepan, lightly toast the pepper, turmeric, ginger and cinnamon to bring out flavor. Careful not to burn. Remove.

Brown the chicken or beef and chopped onion in oil in a nonstick skillet, then transfer to the presoaked clay pot, along with the water and toasted seasoning mixture.

Place covered clay pot in a cold oven. Set oven at 480°F (249°C). Cook 35 minutes, remove from the oven and add the pitted prunes and the zucchini. Sprinkle with the parsley, coriander, thyme, oregano and 3 tbs (45 ml) of the honey.

Cover the pot and return to the oven. Cook an additional 15 minutes, then check to see if the chicken is done; if not, cook an additional 10 minutes.

Meanwhile, peel and core the apples and cut into squares. Sauté the apples and almonds in a nonstick skillet in the butter, along with the remaining honey and a pinch of cinnamon, until the apples are softened, but still slightly firm.

To serve, top the stew with sautéed apples and almonds. Serves 8.

Approximate nutritional analysis per serving:
Calories 557, Protein 53 g, Carbohydrates 60 g, Fat 14 g, Saturated Fat 3 g,
22% of Calories from Fat, Cholesterol 13 mg, Sodium 122 mg

Cut the zucchini into 1-inch lengths.

CHICKEN MEDITERRANEAN

4 chicken legs, skin removed
4 chicken thighs, skin removed
2 chicken breasts, skin removed, halved
1 tbs (15 ml) cornstarch
salt, to taste
pepper, to taste
1 tsp (5 ml) ground ginger
3 cups (720 ml) cooked chick peas, unsalted
1 10-oz pkg (300 g) artichoke hearts
grated rind and juice of 1 lemon
6 cardamom pods
4 bay leaves
2 cups (480 ml) defatted, low-sodium chicken stock
1 ½ tsp (8 ml) walnut or pistachio oil
1 tbs (15 ml) sunflower oil

Soak the top and the bottom of 3-quart (3 l) clay pot in water for 10 minutes; drain.

Dust the chicken pieces with the cornstarch, seasoning and ginger.

Pour the chick peas into the presoaked clay pot. Mix in the artichoke hearts. Arrange the chicken pieces on top, then sprinkle with the lemon rind and juice. Add the cardamom pods and bay leaves. Pour in the stock. Sprinkle the walnut or pistachio oil over the chicken first, then do the same with the sunflower oil.

Cover the clay pot and place in a cold oven. Set the oven at 450°F (230°C). Cook for 50-55 minutes, until the chicken is well done.

Serve at once. Serves 4.

Note: Bean liquid, ½-1 cup (120-240 ml) can be substituted for equal amount chicken stock.

Approximate nutritional analysis per serving:
Calories 417, Protein 41 g, Carbohydrates 41 g, Fat 10 g, Saturated Fat 2 g,
21% of Calories from Fat, Cholesterol 92 mg, Sodium 139 mg

Dust the chicken with the cornstarch, seasoning and ginger.

TURKEY DOPIAZA

2 lbs (910 g) turkey breast
2 tbs (30 ml) ground coriander
1 tsp (5 ml) ground cumin
½ tsp (3 ml) chili powder, optional
salt, optional
pepper, to taste
3 tbs (45 ml) oil
1 lb (455 g) onions, thinly sliced
1 cup (240 ml) low-fat plain yogurt
4 garlic cloves
4 tbs (60 ml) grated fresh ginger root
1 cinnamon stick
4 cloves
6 cardamom pods
2 tbs (30 ml) chopped cilantro
lemon wedges, to serve

Soak the top and the bottom of 3-quart (3 l) clay pot in water for 10 minutes; drain.

Place the turkey in a bowl. Add the coriander, cumin, chili powder (if used) and seasoning. Toss the turkey to coat with the spices and set aside. Heat 2 tbs of the oil in a nonstick skillet. Add two-thirds of the onions and sauté until golden brown.

Meanwhile, purée the remaining oil and onions with the yogurt, garlic and ginger root. Pour this paste over the meat, add the cinnamon, cloves and cardamom pods and mix well. Reserve some of the browned onion for garnish. Layer the rest of the onions and the meat mixture in the presoaked clay pot.

Cover the clay pot and place in a cold oven. Set oven at 400°F (205°C). Cook for 2½ hours, until the meat is tender. Taste for seasoning, then sprinkle the reserved onions over the dopiaza and cook, uncovered, for 10 minutes. Serve garnished with the browned onion and the chopped cilantro. Serve with lemon wedges. Serve with rice. Serves 8.

Approximate nutritional analysis per serving:
Calories 225, Protein 36 g, Carbohydrates 3 g, Fat 7 g, Saturated Fat 1 g,
29% of Calories from Fat, Cholesterol 99 mg, Sodium 84 mg

Pour the yogurt paste over the meat.

ROAST TURKEY

7-10 lb (3.2-4.6 kg) turkey
2 fresh bouquets garnis (an herb bundle containing a few sprigs
   of parsley, thyme and a bay leaf)
2 onions
salt, to taste
pepper, to taste

Giblet Stock:
turkey giblets and neck
1 onion, sliced
1 carrot, sliced
1 bay leaf
salt, optional
pepper, to taste
defatted, low-sodium chicken or turkey stock, if needed

Gravy:
2 cups (480 ml) giblet stock
1 tbs (15 ml) cornstarch
2 tbs (30 ml) water

Soak the top and the bottom of 4¾-quart (4.6 l) clay pot in water for 10 minutes; drain.

Rinse and thoroughly dry the turkey, taking note of its weight. Place one bouquet garni and one onion in the body cavity, then truss the bird neatly. Slice the remaining onion and lay the slices in the presoaked clay pot, salt and pepper to taste. Place the bird on top and add the remaining bouquet garni.

Cover the clay pot and place in a cold oven. Set the oven at 400°F (205°C). Cook for 20 minutes per pound plus an extra 20 minutes.

Giblet Stock: Simmer the turkey neck and giblets with onion, carrot and bay leaf in water to cover for 1 hour. Strain. Reserve. Skim fat from the turkey cooking juices, then pour juices into the saucepan with turkey giblet stock. Reduce by ⅓ to intensify flavor.

Gravy: Add additional chicken or turkey stock to make 2 cups (480 ml) Giblet Stock liquid. Dilute cornstarch in water and add in increments to boiling stock until gravy has reached desired thickness. Simmer for 2 minutes, season and serve with the carved turkey. Serves 14.

Approximate nutritional analysis per serving Roast Turkey w/o Gravy:
Calories 386, Protein 66 g, Carbohydrates 0 g, Fat 0 g, Saturated Fat 4 g,
28% of Calories from Fat, Cholesterol 172 mg, Sodium 159 mg

Approximate nutritional analysis per ⅛ cup serving Gravy:
Calories 5, Protein 0 g, Carbohydrates 1 g, Fat 0 g, Saturated Fat 0 g,
0% of Calories from Fat, Cholesterol 0 mg, Sodium <1 mg

Truss the bird neatly.

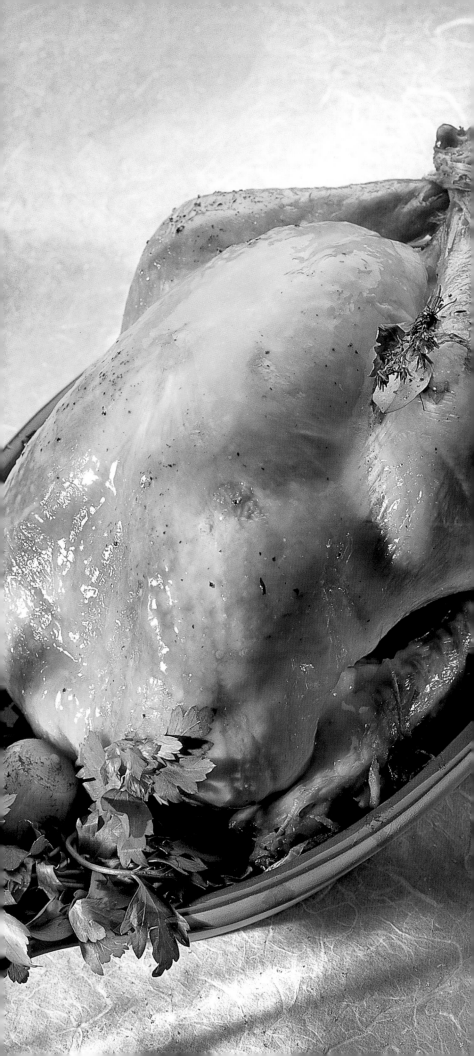

TURKEY "BRISKET" WITH JUNIPER

1 3-lb (1.4 kg) turkey breast
2 tbs (30 ml) all-purpose flour
10 juniper berries, crushed
1 tsp (5 ml) chopped rosemary
1 tsp (5 ml) chopped thyme
1 tsp (5 ml) grated nutmeg
salt, to taste
pepper, to taste
2 tsp (10 ml) cider vinegar
1 tbs (15 ml) brown sugar
1 cup (240 ml) red wine
1 cup (240 ml) water
3 lbs (1.4 kg) pearl onions
1 ½ lbs (685 g) small mushrooms

Soak the top and the bottom of 3-quart (3 l) clay pot in water for 10 minutes; drain.

Place turkey in the presoaked clay pot.

Mix together the flour, juniper berries, rosemary, thyme, nutmeg and salt and pepper. Add the cider vinegar and brown sugar. Rub this seasoning mixture all over the turkey. Pour the red wine into the bottom of the pot and add the water. Add the onions. Cover the clay pot and place in a cold oven. Set the oven at 450°F (230°C). Cook for 20 minutes per pound.

Baste the turkey, add the mushrooms and cook, covered, for another 45 minutes, until the turkey is succulent and tender and the juices run clear. Serve with boiled or mashed potatoes, rice or pasta. Serves 8.

Approximate nutritional analysis per serving:
Calories 339, Protein 55 g, Carbohydrates 22 g, Fat 3 g, Saturated Fat <1 g,
7% of Calories from Fat, Cholesterol 146 mg, Sodium 103 mg

Rub seasoning mixture all over the turkey.

DUCK PROVENÇAL

2 garlic heads
4 duck breasts, skin and visible fat removed
grated rind and juice of 1 lime
6 tbs (90 ml) chopped parsley
4 savory or thyme sprigs
2 blades of mace
1 cinnamon stick
salt, optional
pepper, to taste
¾ lb (340 g) green lentils
1 onion, chopped
2 tbs (30 ml) all-purpose flour
1 cup (240 ml) defatted low-sodium chicken stock

Soak the top and the bottom of 3-quart (3 l) clay pot in water for 10 minutes; drain.

Peel the garlic cloves. Place in a small saucepan and pour in water to cover. Bring to a boil, reduce the heat and cover the pan. Simmer for 20 minutes, then drain.

Prick the duck pieces, place them in the presoaked clay pot and add the garlic cloves around them. Sprinkle with the lime rind, juice and parsley. Add the savory or thyme, mace and cinnamon, tucking them under the duck. Season well.

Cover the clay pot and place in a cold oven. Set oven at 425°F (220°C). Cook for 40 minutes. Meanwhile, place the lentils in a saucepan with water to cover. Add the onion and bring to a boil. Reduce the heat, cover and simmer for 30 minutes. Drain.

Drain the cooking juices from the duck into a saucepan. Skim off the fat.Stir in the flour, heat, then add the stock and bring to a boil, stirring; add seasoning. Set the duck pieces aside, tip the lentils into the clay pot, then place the duck on top. Pour in the sauce. Return clay pot, uncovered, to the oven for another 15 minutes.

Slice breasts and serve on a bed of lentils. Wilted spinach and rice make excellent accompaniments. Serves 4.

Approximate nutritional analysis per serving:
Calories 570, Protein 60 g, Carbohydrates 66 g, Fat 8 g, Saturated Fat 2 g,
13% of Calories from Fat, Cholesterol 128 mg, Sodium 112 mg

Place duck in the clay pot and add the garlic cloves around them.

DUCK BREASTS WITH VEGETABLES

4 boneless duck breasts, skin and visible fat removed
2 tsp (10 ml) walnut or pistachio oil
salt, optional
pepper, to taste
1 tsp (5 ml) paprika
2 tbs (30 ml) chopped mixed herbs
½ lb (230 g) baby corncobs
1 small leek, white part only, sliced
¼ lb (115 g) snow peas
4 tbs (60 ml) dry sherry
3 tbs (45 ml) shelled pistachio nuts, optional
herb sprigs, to garnish

Soak the top and the bottom of 3-quart (3 l) clay pot in water for 10 minutes; drain.

Place the duck portions in the presoaked clay pot. Sprinkle with walnut oil, salt and pepper, paprika and herbs.

Cover the clay pot and place in a cold oven. Set at 450°F (230°C). Cook for 40 minutes.

Meanwhile, add the corn cobs to a small saucepan of boiling water and boil for 3 minutes. Add the leek slices and cook for 1 minute, then add the snow peas, shake the pan and drain at once. Set aside.

Remove the duck from the clay pot. Skim off the fat. Tip in all the vegetables, toss them in the cooking juices, then replace the duck on top. Sprinkle the sherry over it all and top the duck with the nuts. Return the pot, uncovered, to the oven and cook for another 15 minutes.

Garnish with herb sprigs and serve at once with fresh noodles, couscous or a mixture of wild rice and basmati rice. Serves 4.

Approximate nutritional analysis per serving:
Calories 322 Protein 37 g, Carbohydrates 19 g, Fat 10 g, Saturated Fat 3 g,
29% of Calories from Fat, Cholesterol 128 mg, Sodium 110 mg

Skin and remove fat from duck breasts.

LOW-FAT SHEPHERD'S PIE

1 tsp (5 ml) oil
1 large onion, chopped
½ lb (230 g) ground turkey
1 cup (240 ml) pinto beans
1 carrot, diced
¼ lb (115 g) mushrooms, sliced
1 tsp (5 ml) dried mixed herbs
salt, optional
pepper, to taste
2 tbs (30 ml) all-purpose flour
1½ cups (355 ml) defatted, low-sodium chicken stock
1½ lbs (685 g) potatoes, boiled and mashed
1 tbs (15 ml) reduced-fat margarine
parsley sprigs, to garnish, optional

Soak the top and the bottom of 3-quart (3 l) clay pot in water for 10 minutes; drain.

Heat the oil in a large nonstick skillet. Add the onion and cook for 5 minutes, then stir in the ground turkey and cook until lightly browned. Add the pinto beans, carrot, mushrooms, herbs and seasoning. Stir in the flour; continue stirring while adding the stock. Turn the turkey mixture into the presoaked clay pot.

Cover the turkey mixture with the mashed potatoes and score the top with a fork. Dot with margarine.

Cover the clay pot and place in a cold oven. Set oven at 450°F (230°C).

Cook for 30 minutes. Uncover the clay pot and cook for an additional 15 minutes.

Serve piping hot, garnished with parsley. Serves 6.

Approximate nutritional analysis per serving:
Calories 278, Protein 17 g, Carbohydrates 36 g, Fat 8 g, Saturated Fat 2 g,
26% of Calories from Fat, Cholesterol 26 mg, Sodium 83 mg

Cover the turkey mixture with the mashed potatoes.

TURKEY CHILI

1 lb (455 g) lean turkey breast, diced
2 tbs (30 ml) all-purpose flour
2 tsp (10 ml) ground cumin
1 tsp (5 ml) oregano
salt, optional
pepper, to taste
1 tbs (15 ml) olive oil
2 garlic cloves, crushed
2 onions, halved and sliced
2-4 canned jalapeño chilies, chopped*
3 cups (720 ml) low-sodium white (cannellini or navy) beans, drained
1 cup (240 ml) vegetable stock
1 avocado, optional
2 tbs (30 ml) chopped cilantro
1 tbs (15 ml) chopped mint
1 lime, cut in wedges

Soak the top and the bottom of 3-quart (3 l) clay pot in water for 10 minutes; drain.

Cover the turkey with a coating of flour, cumin, oregano and plenty of seasoning. Heat the oil in a nonstick skillet and quickly brown the turkey. Add the garlic and onions and cook for 2 minutes, then turn the mixture into a presoaked clay pot. Add the chilies, beans and stock.

Cover the clay pot and place in a cold oven. Set oven at 450°F (230°C). Cook for 1 hour. When the chili is cooked, halve, pit and peel the avocado, then slice it.

Top each portion of chili with cilantro, mint and avocado. Serve lime wedges for their juice. Serves 4.

*Note: Make the chili as hot as you like by adding more jalapeños. Canned jalapeños are quite mild and a whole, small can will not make the dish too fiery. Fresh chilies are very hot.

Approximate nutritional analysis per serving:
Calories 437, Protein 48 g, Carbohydrates 48 g, Fat 6 g, Saturated Fat 1 g,
12% of Calories from Fat, Cholesterol 97 mg, Sodium 122 mg

Turn the mixture into a presoaked clay pot.

MEAT

TUSCAN VEAL STEW

**2 lbs (910 g) stewing veal
    or 6 pieces veal shanks or shinbones
3 tbs (45 ml) all-purpose flour
salt, optional
pepper, to taste
2 tbs (15 ml) oil
1 onion, halved and sliced
2 garlic cloves, crushed
1 bay leaf
1 cup (240 ml) dry white wine
1 cup (240 ml) chicken stock
1 lb (455 g) tomatoes, peeled and chopped
4 tbs (60 ml) chopped parsley
grated rind of 1 lemon**

Soak the top and bottom of a 3-quart (3 l) clay pot in water for 10 minutes; drain.

Toss the veal with the flour and salt and pepper to taste. Heat the oil in a nonstick skillet and brown the meat. Transfer the meat to the presoaked clay pot. Add the onion, half the garlic and the bay leaf to the skillet and cook for 5 minutes. Stir in the wine, stock and tomatoes. Mix well and pour into the clay pot.

Cover the clay pot and place in a cold oven. Set the oven at 400°F (205°C). Cook for 2½ hours.

Mix together the remaining garlic, parsley and lemon rind. Taste the casserole for seasoning, sprinkle with the parsley mixture and serve. Serves 6.

Note: When the stew is made with veal shanks or shin bones it is called osso buco. Arrange the meat so that the bones stand cut side upright to retain the flavorsome marrow. The lemon, garlic and parsley mixture is called gremolada.

Approximate nutritional analysis per serving:
Calories 335, Protein 45 g, Carbohydrates 11 g, Fat 10 g, Saturated Fat 3 g,
29% of Calories from Fat, Cholesterol 158 mg, Sodium 138 mg

Finely grate the rind of 1 lemon.

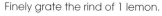

LOW-FAT POT ROAST

1 3-lb (1.4 kg) eye of round in one piece
salt, optional
pepper, to taste
3 large onions, thickly sliced
6 carrots, thickly sliced
3 parsnips, thickly sliced
½ tsp (3 ml) ground mace
1 bouquet garni, an herb bundle containing a few sprigs of parsley,
thyme and a bay leaf
2 cups (480 ml) stout or dark ale
1 cup (240 ml) water
8 large potatoes, quartered

Soak the top and the bottom of 3-quart (3 l) clay pot in water for 10 minutes; drain.

Tie the meat into a neat shape, then season it with salt and pepper to taste. Sprinkle the onions over the base of the presoaked clay pot. Top with a layer of carrots and another of parsnips. Add the mace and bouquet garni, then place the meat on top of the herbs. Pour in the stout and the water.

Cover the pot and place in a cold oven. Set the oven at 450°F (230°C). Cook for 1½ hours. Baste the meat well and add the potatoes to the clay pot, arranging them around the meat. Cook for another 45 minutes until the potatoes are tender and the meat is cooked through.

Transfer the meat to a serving plate with the vegetables. Skim fat from cooking liquid and strain into a sauce boat and serve separately. Serves 8.

Approximate nutritional analysis per serving:
Calories 515, Protein 54 g, Carbohydrates 49 g, Fat 10 g, Saturated Fat 4 g,
18% of Calories from Fat, Cholesterol 117 mg, Sodium 158 mg

Thickly slice the vegetables.

BEEF BURGUNDY

2 lbs (910 g) stewing beef, cubed
1 bouquet garni, an herb bundle containing a few sprigs of parsley,
**   thyme and a bay leaf**
2 garlic cloves, crushed
salt and pepper, to taste
1 bottle red wine
4 slices bacon, diced
1 tbs (15 ml) oil
¾ lb (340 g) pearl onions
4 tbs (60 ml) brandy
1 tbs (15 ml) cornstarch
2 tbs (30 ml) water
½ lb (230 g) small mushrooms
3 tbs (45 ml) chopped parsley
herb sprigs and croutons, to garnish

Place the stewing beef in a bowl. Add the bouquet garni, garlic, and seasoning to taste, then pour in the wine. Cover and chill for 24 hours.

Soak the top and the bottom of 3-quart (3 l) clay pot in water for 10 minutes; drain. Drain the meat, reserving the marinade. Blanch bacon in boiling water for 2 minutes, drain, pat dry. Heat the oil, brown the onions in a nonstick skillet, then transfer to the presoaked clay pot.

Brown the meat, pour in the brandy and set it alight. When the flames subside, pour the meat and juices into the clay pot. Add the marinade. Cover the clay pot and place in a cold oven. Set oven at 450°F (230°C). Cook for 2 hours.

Mix cornstarch and water. Gradually stir this into the meat mixture. Add the mushrooms. Cook, covered, for another 30 minutes. Taste for seasoning.

Sprinkle with chopped parsley and garnish with herb sprigs and croûtons. Serve with noodles and a crisp green salad. Serves 6.

Approximate nutritional analysis per serving:
Calories 451 Protein 50 g, Carbohydrates 12 g, Fat 14 g, Saturated Fat 4 g,
28% of Calories from Fat, Cholesterol 147 mg, Sodium 130 mg

The ingredients.

BEEF ORIENTAL

1 lb (455 g) braising steak, finely diced
1 green chili pepper, seeded and chopped
1 garlic clove, crushed
¼ tsp (1 ml) ground allspice
½ tsp (3 ml) ground ginger
4 tbs (60 ml) raisins
2 large onions, finely chopped
juice of ½ lemon
2 tbs (30 ml) mango chutney, chopped
salt, optional
pepper, to taste
1 cup (240 ml) water
1½ lbs (685 g) sweet potatoes, diced
1 firm mango, peeled and diced
1 tbs (15 ml) chopped mint
1 head of iceberg lettuce, separated into leaves

Place the beef in a bowl. Add the chili pepper, garlic, allspice, ginger, raisins, onions, lemon juice and mango chutney. Sprinkle in seasoning, mix thoroughly and leave to marinate for at least 1 hour. The mixture may be chilled overnight.

Soak the top and the bottom of 3-quart (3 l) clay pot in water for 10 minutes; drain. Turn mixture into the presoaked clay pot and add the water.

Cover the clay pot and place in a cold oven. Set oven at 425°F (220°C). Cook for 30 minutes. Stir in the sweet potato and cook, covered, for another 30 minutes. Finally, add the mango and cook, covered, for another 30 minutes, until the meat is really succulent. The mixture should be juicy, neither watery nor too dry, so add a little extra hot water if necessary.

Mix in the mint lightly before serving. The mixture is eaten by spooning some onto a lettuce leaf, folding the leaf and munching through the package. Serves 6.

Approximate nutritional analysis per serving:
Calories 348, Protein 27 g, Carbohydrates 49 g, Fat 6 g, Saturated Fat 2 g,
14% of Calories from Fat, Cholesterol 73 mg, Sodium 55 mg

Prepare the fruits and vegetables.

CASSOULET

2 cups (480 ml) dried small white beans, rinsed
2 slices lean bacon, chopped
1 medium onion, diced
2 medium carrots, diced
1 large celery rib, diced
½ cup (120 ml) dry white wine
1½ cups (355 ml) defatted, low-sodium chicken stock
8 garlic cloves, chopped
1 bay leaf
4 sprigs thyme or ¼ tsp (1 ml) dried thyme leaves
6 whole peppercorns
1½ cups (355 ml) low-salt chopped tomatoes with juice
1½ lbs (685 g) boneless lamb shoulder, trimmed, cut in small cubes
½ lb (230 g) smoked turkey sausage
4 sprigs parsley
1 tbs (15 ml) olive oil
1½ cups (355 ml) fresh French bread crumbs

Place beans in a saucepan and cover with water plus 1 inch; bring to a boil; boil for 5 minutes. Let stand for 55 minutes. Drain. Or soak in cold water for 8 hours or overnight.

Soak the top and the bottom of 3-quart (3 l) clay pot in water for 10 minutes; drain. Blanch bacon in boiling water for 30 seconds. Drain, rinse and pat dry.

Place all ingredients except parsley, olive oil and bread crumbs in clay pot.

Place clay pot in a cold oven. Set oven at 375°F (190°C). Bake, stirring once or twice, until beans and lamb are very tender, about 3 hours. Check to make sure the liquid fully covers the beans. Remove sausage and cut into 1½-inch (3.75 cm) pieces; return to clay pot. Toast bread crumbs in olive oil in nonstick skillet. Sprinkle evenly with bread crumbs. Bake uncovered until sausage is hot and bread crumbs are crisp and brown, about 35 minutes. Serves 8

Approximate nutritional analysis per serving:
Calories 544, Protein 41 g, Carbohydrates 55 g, Fat 17 g, Saturated Fat 6 g,
29% of Calories from Fat, Cholesterol 95 mg, Sodium 470 mg

Dice the vegetables.

MIDDLE EASTERN STUFFED PEPPERS

Sauce:
4 large ripe tomatoes, chopped coarsely
2 large onions, chopped fine
¼ cup (60 ml) water
½ tsp (3 ml) salt
½ tsp (3 ml) freshly ground pepper
1 tsp (5 ml) dried oregano
1 cup (240 ml) pinto beans, fresh or canned

Peppers and Stuffing:
6 green peppers
1 lb (455 g) lean ground lamb
2 tbs (30 ml) chopped fresh mint or 1 tbs (15 ml) dried mint
1 clove garlic, crushed
1 small onion, chopped fine
½ tsp (3 ml) fresh grated nutmeg
½ tsp (3 ml) ground allspice
½ tsp (3 ml) salt
½ tsp (3 ml) freshly ground pepper
¾ cup (180 ml) slightly undercooked rice

Soak the top and the bottom of 3-quart (3 l) clay pot in water for 10 minutes; drain.

Sauce: Place all ingredients, except the pinto beans, into a saucepan and bring to a boil. Reduce the heat, cover the pan and simmer slowly for 20 minutes.

Peppers and Stuffing: Meanwhile, remove tops of the peppers and take out the seeds and white pulp. Mix all ingredients for the stuffing and stuff the peppers. Place the stuffed peppers in the presoaked clay pot, pour the Sauce over and add the pinto beans.

Place the covered clay pot in a cold oven. Set oven at 450°F (230°C). Cook for 50-60 minutes, testing the beans for doneness. Serves 6.

Approximate nutritional analysis per serving:
Calories 322, Protein 28 g, Carbohydrates 34 g, Fat 8 g, Saturated Fat 3 g,
23% of Calories from Fat, Cholesterol 72 mg, Sodium 434 mg

Mix all ingredients for the stuffing and stuff the peppers.

LAMB-STUFFED CABBAGE LEAVES

12-16 large cabbage leaves (1 or 2 heads)
½ cup (120 ml) water
salt, optional
1 cup (240 ml) chopped cabbage
1 cup (240 ml) ground lamb
1 cup (240 ml) ground beef, lean or extra lean
1 medium onion, grated
¼ tsp (1 ml) grated nutmeg
½ tsp (3 ml) salt
¼ tsp (1 ml) freshly ground black pepper
1 cup (240 ml) whole wheat bread crumbs,
**   moistened in 1 tbs (15 ml) olive oil**
¼ cup (60 ml) dark molasses
¼ cup (60 ml) red wine
1 tbs (15 ml) olive oil, optional
1 tsp (5 ml) arrowroot

Soak the top and the bottom of 3-quart (3 l) clay pot in water for 10 minutes; drain.

Steam cabbage leaves in ½ cup salted water for 3-4 minutes. Drain and set aside.

Combine chopped cabbage with all the other ingredients except the molasses, wine, olive oil and arrowroot. Place a heaping tablespoon of the mixture in center of each cabbage leaf, roll up and place in the presoaked clay pot.

Combine molasses, wine and olive oil and pour over the stuffed cabbage leaves.

Cover the clay pot and place in a cold oven. Set the oven at 475°F (245°C). Cook for 70 minutes.

When done, remove the clay pot from the oven and pour off the sauce into a saucepan. Bring to a boil and thicken with the arrowroot mixed with a little water.

Pour sauce over the cabbage rolls and serve. Serves 4.

Note: You can use 2 cups (480 ml) ground lamb and omit the beef, if preferred.

Approximate nutritional analysis per serving:
Calories 300, Protein 17 g, Carbohydrates 41 g, Fat 8 g, Saturated Fat 3 g,
24% of Calories from Fat, Cholesterol 43 mg, Sodium 530 mg

Place a heaping tablespoon of the mixture in center of each cabbage leaf.

MOUSSAKA WITH TOMATO SAUCE

2 1¼-lb (570 g each) eggplants, unpared
olive or salad oil, optional
2 eggs
    or ½ cup (120 l) egg substitute
1 cup (240 ml) fresh bread crumbs
1 large onion, finely chopped
2 cloves garlic, minced
2 tsp (10 ml) paprika
½ tsp (3 ml) salt
½ tsp (3 ml) dried rosemary leaves, crumbled
2 lbs (910 g) ground lamb
1 batch Tomato Sauce with Mushrooms (below)
parsley sprigs, to garnish

Tomato Sauce with Mushrooms:
1 large onion, finely chopped
1 tbs (15 ml) olive oil
¼ lb (115 g) mushrooms, sliced
16-oz can (480 g) salt-free tomatoes, coarsely chopped,
    liquid reserved
½ cup (120 ml) defatted, low-sodium, regular-strength
    chicken stock, homemade or canned
½ tsp (3 ml) salt
¼ tsp (1 ml) white pepper
¼ tsp (1 ml) dried oregano leaves
¼ tsp (1 ml) sugar

Soak the top and the bottom of 3-quart (3 l) clay pot in water for 10 minutes; drain.

Preheat oven to 375°F (190°C) to cook eggplant.

Cut stems from eggplants; cut lengthwise into halves. Place eggplant flesh side down, on a lightly oiled baking sheet (or one lined with nonstick baking parchment). Bake for 30 minutes or until very soft. Let both the eggplant and the oven cool.

Carefully scrape eggplant flesh from skins; leave skins intact and cut the skin in half again. Brush eggplant skins on both sides with olive oil. Line bottom and sides of presoaked clay pot with skins, dark sides down. Coarsely chop the eggplant flesh into ½-inch (1.25 cm) pieces.

Beat eggs lightly; stir in bread crumbs, onion, garlic, paprika, salt and the rosemary. Add lamb and chopped eggplant. Spread mixture in clay pot.

Place covered clay pot in a cold oven. Set oven at 425°F (220°C). Bake until lamb is firm in center and top is brown, about 1¾ hours. Spoon off and discard fat. Let stand covered 5 minutes.

While Moussaka is baking, make Tomato Sauce with Mushrooms. Sauté onion in olive oil in a nonstick skillet until soft. Stir in mushrooms; sauté until light brown. Combine with remaining ingredients in a 2-quart (1.9 l) saucepan. Heat to boiling; reduce heat. Simmer, covered, for 15 minutes. Remove cover; cook over medium-high heat, stirring occasionally, until thick, about 30 minutes.

Loosen edges of Moussaka with spatula. Invert onto warm serving platter. Spoon some tomato sauce over the top. Garnish with parsley. Cut into thick slices and serve with remaining tomato sauce. Serves 10.

Note: The butcher can grind a fat-trimmed lamb shoulder cut for a lean ground lamb.

Approximate nutritional analysis per serving:
Calories 387, Protein 28 g, Carbohydrates 28 g, Fat 18 g, Saturated Fat 5 g,
42% of Calories from Fat, Cholesterol 122 mg, Sodium 373 mg

Cut stems from eggplants; cut lengthwise into halves.

PORK WITH HONEY AND ALMONDS

**2 lbs (910 g) boneless pork loin, trimmed of fat and
  cut into large chunks
2 large onions, chopped fine
3 tbs (45 ml) honey
1 cup (240 ml) raisins
4 carrots, peeled and cut into 1-inch (2.5 cm) lengths
½ cup (120 ml) slivered almonds
pinch saffron powder
  or ½ tsp (3 ml) saffron threads
1 tsp (5 ml) cinnamon
½ tsp (3 ml) ground ginger
pinch of cayenne pepper
2 cups (480 ml) garbanzo beans, unsalted, with their liquid
½ cup (120 ml) water
1 tsp (5 ml) arrowroot, approximately**

Soak the top and the bottom of 3-quart (3 l) clay pot in water for 10 minutes; drain.

Pour all ingredients, except arrowroot, into a large round bowl and mix thoroughly with your hands. Place mixture in the presoaked clay pot.

Place the covered clay pot in a cold oven. Set oven at 450°F (230°C). Cook for 90 minutes. Remove clay pot from oven, pour off liquid into a saucepan, bring it almost to a boil, and thicken with arrowroot.

Serve with brown rice or bulgur. Pour the sauce over both the rice and the pork. Serves 6.

Approximate nutritional analysis per serving:
Calories 414, Protein 39 g, Carbohydrates 60 g, Fat 9 g, Saturated Fat 2 g,
18% of Calories from Fat, Cholesterol 84 mg, Sodium 105 mg

Chop 2 large onions finely.

CHILE VERDE

**6-12 fresh jalapeño peppers, seeds removed and chopped
  into ¼-inch (.625 cm) dice
  or 2 4-oz cans (240 g) peeled green chili peppers (if you want it mild)**
3 lbs (1.4 kg) pork loin or tenderloin, cut into ½-inch (1.25 cm) cubes
6 large cloves garlic, crushed
1 cup (240 ml) defatted low-sodium beef stock
½ tsp (3 ml) cumin
¾ cup (180 ml) beer
3-inch (7.5 cm) strip orange peel
½ tsp (3 ml) salt
1 tbs (15 ml) chopped cilantro, to garnish
1 cup (240 ml) diced fresh tomatoes, to garnish
½ tbs (3 ml) diced red onion, to garnish
4 tbs (60 ml) reduced-fat sour cream, to garnish

Soak the top and the bottom of 3-quart (3 l) clay pot in water for 10 minutes; drain.

Mix all the ingredients together, except the garnish items, and place in the presoaked clay pot.

Place the covered clay pot in a cold oven. Set oven at 450°F (230°C). Cook for 90 minutes. Meanwhile, combine garnish ingredients, except sour cream, in a bowl.

Serve in soup bowls garnished with tomato garnish and a dollop of sour cream. Serves 6-8.

Approximate nutritional analysis per serving:
Calories 371, Protein 49 g, Carbohydrates 3 g, Fat 17 g, Saturated Fat 6 g,
42% of Calories from Fat, Cholesterol 151 mg, Sodium 242 mg

Chop cilantro for a sprightly garnish.

PORK CHOPS MEXICALI

1 tsp (5 ml) oil
1 large onion, chopped
3 cups (720 ml) cubed pumpkin flesh
1 tsp (5 ml) ground cinnamon
grated nutmeg
salt, optional
pepper, to taste
4 pork chops, visible fat removed
4 sprigs rosemary
grated rind and juice of 1 orange
halved orange slices, to garnish

Soak the top and the bottom of 3-quart (3 l) clay pot in water for 10 minutes; drain.

Heat the oil in a large nonstick skillet. Add onion and cook for 2 minutes, stir in the pumpkin, then turn the mixture into the presoaked clay pot. Sprinkle with cinnamon, a little grated nutmeg and salt and pepper to taste. Lay the pork chops on top and tuck the rosemary in between them. Season the chops, then pour the orange juice and rind over.

Cover the clay pot and place in a cold oven. Set oven at 450°F (230°C). Cook for 1 hour. Baste the chops with the cooking juices and cook, uncovered, for another 5-10 minutes.

Garnish with orange slices and the rosemary sprigs used in cooking. Baked potatoes topped with low-fat plain yogurt or low-fat sour cream taste terrific with the slightly spicy pork and pumpkin. Serves 4.

Approximate nutritional analysis per serving:
Calories 274, Protein 26 g, Carbohydrates 24 g, Fat 9 g, Saturated Fat 3 g,
29% of Calories from Fat, Cholesterol 71 mg, Sodium 61 mg

Oranges are used for both flavoring and garnish.

VEGETABLES

BRAISED BELGIAN ENDIVE

1 lb (455 g) small Belgian endives
1 tsp (5 ml) olive oil
2 tsp (10 ml) lemon juice
salt, optional
white pepper, to taste
1 cup (240 ml) defatted, low-sodium chicken stock,
**   canned or homemade**

Soak top and bottom of 5½ cup/2-quart (1.3-1.9 l) clay pot in water about 10 minutes; drain.

Trim ends of endives and remove discolored outer leaves. Place endives in presoaked clay pot. Sprinkle with olive oil, lemon juice, salt and pepper. Pour in chicken stock.

Place covered clay pot in a cold oven. Set oven at 425°F (220°C). Bake until endives are tender, about 45 minutes. Pour cooking liquid into medium saucepan; cover clay pot to keep endive warm. Heat cooking liquid to boiling; cook, stirring occasionally, until syrupy.

Pour sauce over endive. Serves 4.

Approximate nutritional analysis per serving:
Calories 35, Protein 2 g, Carbohydrates 5 g, Fat 1 g, Saturated Fat <1 g,
33% of Calories from Fat, Cholesterol 0 mg, Sodium 26 mg

Endives are a perfect winter vegetable.

SWISS CHARD WITH ONION

2 medium onions, thinly sliced, separated into rings
1 tbs (15 ml) olive oil
2 cloves garlic, minced
1 lb (455 g) Swiss chard, coarsely chopped
salt, optional
pepper, to taste
1 tsp (5 ml) lemon juice

Soak top and bottom of 3-quart (3 l) clay pot in water about 10 minutes; drain.

Sauté onions in olive oil in large nonstick skillet over medium heat, stirring occasionally, until limp and beginning to brown; stir in garlic. Spread onion mixture in bottom of pot. Add chard.

Place covered clay pot in a cold oven. Set oven at 425°F (220°C). Bake, stirring once, until chard is crisp-tender, 20-25 minutes. Season with salt, pepper and lemon juice. Serves 4.

Approximate nutritional analysis per serving:
Calories 100, Protein 4 g, Carbohydrates 15 g, Fat 4 g, Saturated Fat <1 g,
31% of Calories from Fat, Cholesterol 0 mg, Sodium 245 mg

Spread onion mixture in bottom of pot. Add chard.

CABBAGE-POTATO TIAN

1 ½ lbs (685 g) cabbage, shredded
2 onions, thinly sliced
4 large potatoes, peeled and thinly sliced
¼ lb (115 g) Canadian bacon slices, diced
2 bay leaves
salt, optional
pepper, to taste
1 cup (240 ml) skim milk
1 tbs (15 ml) low-fat margarine or butter
1 tbs (15 ml) chopped chives, for garnish

Soak top and bottom of 3-quart (3 l) clay pot in water about 10 minutes; drain.

Layer the cabbage, onions, potatoes and bacon in the presoaked clay pot, ending with a layer of potato on top. Add the bay leaves somewhere around the middle of the clay pot and season the layers well. Pour the milk over.

Cover the clay pot and place in a cold oven. Set oven at 425°F (220°C). Cook for 1 hour. Brush the potatoes with margarine or butter and cook uncovered, for another 15 minutes or until golden brown. Garnish with chopped chives. Serves 4.

Note: Thinly sliced smoked low-fat turkey sausage is delicious layered with the potatoes. Or eliminate meat altogether for a leaner version of the dish.

Approximate nutritional analysis per serving w/ meat:
Calories 199, Protein 12 g, Carbohydrates 29 g, Fat 4 g, Saturated Fat 1 g,
21% of Calories from Fat, Cholesterol 15 mg, Sodium 506 mg

Approximate nutritional analysis per serving w/o meat:
Calories 155, Protein 7 g, Carbohydrates 28 g, Fat 3 g, Saturated Fat <1 g,
15% of Calories from Fat, Cholesterol 1 mg, Sodium 106 mg

Layer the cabbage, onions, potatoes and bacon.

POTATOES WITH PINE NUTS

2 lbs (910 g) small new potatoes, scrubbed
2 small red onions, thinly sliced
2 tbs (30 ml) currants
3 tbs (45 ml) pine nuts
1 tbs (15 ml) olive oil
2 garlic cloves, crushed
10 black olives, pitted and sliced
1 bay leaf
salt, optional
pepper, to taste
½ cup (120 ml) red vermouth
2 tbs (30 ml) shredded basil, approximately
basil sprigs, to garnish

Soak top and bottom of 3-quart (3 l) clay pot in water about 10 minutes; drain.

Place the potatoes in the presoaked clay pot. Mix in the onions, currants, pine nuts and olive oil. Add the garlic, olives and bay leaf with salt and pepper to taste. Pour in the vermouth.

Cover the clay pot and place in a cold oven. Set oven at 450°F (230°C). Cook for 1 hour or until the potatoes are tender. Remove from oven and leave the potatoes to stand in the clay pot, without removing the lid, for 10 minutes.

Mix in the shredded basil and garnish with the whole sprigs. Serves 6.

Approximate nutritional analysis per serving:
Calories 224, Protein 5 g, Carbohydrates 40 g, Fat 6 g, Saturated Fat <1 g,
23% of Calories from Fat, Cholesterol 0 mg, Sodium 74 mg

Olives and basil give this dish a Mediterranean twist.

MIDDLE EASTERN POTATOES WITH PEAS

2 lbs (910 g) small new potatoes, scrubbed
1 large onion, chopped
2 tbs (30 ml) cumin seeds
2 tbs (30 ml) oil or melted ghee
juice of 1 lemon
salt, optional
pepper, to taste
½ lb (230 g) frozen peas
2 tbs (30 ml) chopped mint

Soak top and bottom of 3-quart (3 l) clay pot in water about 10 minutes; drain.

Place the potatoes in the presoaked clay pot. Add onion, cumin seeds, oil and lemon juice. Add salt and pepper to taste.

Cover the clay pot and place in a cold oven. Set oven at 475°F (246°C). Cook for 40 minutes. Add the peas to the clay pot, mixing them with the potatoes. Cook, covered, for another 15 minutes or until the potatoes are tender and the peas are lightly cooked. Let stand for 10 minutes, without removing the lid.

Mix in the mint and serve. Serves 6.

Approximate nutritional analysis per serving:
Calories 207, Protein 4 g, Carbohydrates 38 g, Fat 5 g, Saturated Fat <1 g,
21% of Calories from Fat, Cholesterol 0 mg, Sodium 11 mg

Simple ingredients make a luscious combination.

RICE PILAF

1 onion, chopped
1 green pepper, chopped
1 clove garlic, crushed
1 tbs (15 ml) olive oil
2 tomatoes, chopped
pinch of saffron
2 cups (480 ml) defatted, low-sodium chicken stock
1 cup (240 ml) raw long-grain rice
¼ cup (60 ml) pine nuts
⅓ cup (80 ml) currants or white raisins
½ tsp (3 ml) salt
pinch of freshly ground pepper

Soak top and bottom of 3-quart (3 l) clay pot in water about 10 minutes; drain.

In a saucepan, sauté the chopped onion, green pepper and garlic in the olive oil until transparent and tender. Add the tomatoes and set aside.

Add saffron to the chicken stock and place it in the presoaked clay pot. Add the rice and stir, then add the pine nuts, currants or raisins, salt, pepper and the sautéed vegetable mixture. Stir thoroughly.

Cover the clay pot and place in a cold oven. Set oven at 480°F (249°C). Cook for 45 minutes or until the rice is tender.

Serves 4 as a substantial side dish.

Approximate nutritional analysis per serving:
Calories 353, Protein 8 g, Carbohydrates 61 g, Fat 10 g, Saturated Fat 1 g,
23% of Calories from Fat, Cholesterol 0 mg, Sodium 282 mg

Add saffron to chicken stock and place it in the clay pot.

ORANGE-GLAZED CARROTS

1 ½ lbs (685 g) carrots, cut into fingers
1 tbs (15 ml) brown sugar
salt, optional
pepper, to taste
juice of 1 orange
1 ½ tbs (25 ml) melted butter
1 tbs (15 ml) chopped tarragon
2 tbs (30 ml) snipped chives
tarragon sprigs, to garnish, optional

Soak top and bottom of 3-quart (3 l) clay pot in water about 10 minutes; drain.

Place the carrots in the presoaked clay pot. Sprinkle the brown sugar, salt and pepper over the carrots, then pour in the orange juice. Add the melted butter.

Cover the clay pot and place in a cold oven. Set oven at 425°F (220°C). Cook for 25 minutes. Stir the carrots and cook, uncovered, for another 10 minutes.

Sprinkle with the herbs and garnish with optional tarragon sprigs. Serve at once. Serves 4.

Approximate nutritional analysis per serving:
Calories 128, Protein 2 g, Carbohydrates 24 g, Fat 3 g, Saturated Fat 2 g,
22% of Calories from Fat, Cholesterol 8 mg, Sodium 113 mg

Cut the carrots into quarters or eighths lengthwise.

BUTTERNUT SQUASH CASSEROLE

2 small butternut squash
2 tsp (10 ml) melted butter
1 tbs (15 ml) lemon juice
salt, optional
pepper, to taste
2 tsp (10 ml) walnut oil
2 tsp (10 ml) dry sherry
4 tbs (60 ml) chopped parsley
2 tbs (30 ml) snipped chives
2 tbs (30 ml) chopped walnuts
2 tbs (30 ml) fresh bread crumbs
2 tbs (30 ml) grated Parmesan cheese
parsley sprigs, to garnish

Soak top and bottom of 3-quart (3 l) clay pot in water about 10 minutes; drain.

Cut the squash in half lengthwise. Scoop any small amount of fiber from the central hole, then place the squash halves in the presoaked clay pot with the flesh sides up. Pour the butter and lemon juice over the cut surface of each half, then season lightly.

Cover the clay pot and place in a cold oven. Set the oven at 425°F (220°C). Cook for 45 minutes.

Mix the walnut oil and sherry with the parsley and chives. Spoon this over the squash halves. Sprinkle with the walnuts, bread crumbs and Parmesan and cook, uncovered, for another 15 minutes, or until the topping is crisp and golden and the squash is tender.

Serve garnished with parsley. Serves 4 as a substantial side dish.

Approximate nutritional analysis per serving:
Calories 214, Protein 6 g, Carbohydrates 36 g, Fat 8 g, Saturated Fat 2 g,
30% of Calories from Fat, Cholesterol 8 mg, Sodium 95 mg

Scoop any small amount of fiber from the central hole.

BUTTER BEAN DELIGHT

½ lb (230 g) dried butter beans, soaked overnight
1 bay leaf
1 sprig thyme
1 tbs (15 ml) chopped sage
¼ tsp (1 ml) ground mace
2 carrots, thickly sliced
2 celery stalks, sliced
2 onions, halved and thinly sliced
2½ cups (590 ml) defatted, unsalted chicken or vegetable stock
pepper, to taste
1 cup (240 ml) fresh bread crumbs
½ cup (120 ml) grated reduced fat cheese, such as cheddar

Soak top and bottom of 3-quart (3 l) clay pot in water about 10 minutes; drain.

Drain the beans, place in a saucepan well covered with cold water and bring to a boil. Boil rapidly for 10 minutes, then drain and place in the presoaked clay pot. Add herbs, mace, carrots, celery and onions, in that order without mixing the ingredients. Pour in the stock.

Cover the clay pot and place in a cold oven. Set oven at 425°F (220°C). Cook for 1-1¼ hours or until the beans are tender. Add the seasoning to taste and stir the beans with the vegetables.

Mix the bread crumbs and cheese together and sprinkle the mixture over the top. Cook, uncovered, for another 15 minutes, to brown the topping before serving. Serves 6.

Note: If salt or seasoned stock is used, the beans will become tough and will not soften no matter how long they are cooked.

Approximate nutritional analysis per serving:
Calories 276, Protein 15 g, Carbohydrates 48 g, Fat 3 g, Saturated Fat 1 g,
10% of Calories from Fat, Cholesterol 7 mg, Sodium 237 mg

Slice the vegetables thinly.

COUSCOUS WITH VEGETABLES

1 onion, chopped
1 sweet red pepper, seeded and chopped
1 tbs (15 ml) olive oil
½ lb (230 g) leanest ground beef
2 tbs (30 ml) pine nuts, optional
1 lb (455 g) zucchini, cut in chunks
1 14-oz can (420 g) salt-free chopped tomatoes
salt, to taste
pepper, to taste
¼ tsp (1 ml) red pepper flakes
½ lb (230 g) couscous
3 tbs (45 ml) grated Parmesan cheese
3 tbs (45 ml) dry white bread crumbs

Soak top and bottom of 3-quart (3 l) clay pot in water about 10 minutes; drain.

Mix the onion, sweet red pepper and olive oil in the presoaked clay pot. Add the beef and pine nuts. Mix well, breaking up the meat.

Place the clay pot, uncovered, in a cold oven. Set the oven at 450°F (230°C). Cook for 20 minutes. Stir in the zucchini, tomatoes, seasoning and red pepper flakes and cook, covered, for another 20 minutes.

Meanwhile, put the couscous in a bowl and pour enough boiling water to cover it by 1 inch (2.5 cm). Leave to stand for 20 minutes. Spread the couscous over the top of the beef and zucchini mixture in an even layer. Mix the Parmesan and bread crumbs together and sprinkle over the top. Cook, uncovered, for 10 minutes to brown the top before serving. Serves 6.

Approximate nutritional analysis per serving:
Calories 344, Protein 20 g, Carbohydrates 41 g, Fat 11 g, Saturated Fat 4 g,
29% of Calories from Fat, Cholesterol 40 mg, Sodium 120 mg

Prepare all the ingredients beforehand.

MEATY BUCKWHEAT PILAF

1 tbs (15 ml) oil
1 onion, chopped
1 garlic clove, crushed
¼ lb (60 ml) ready-to-eat dried apricots, roughly chopped
2 tbs (30 ml) sultanas
½ lb (230 g) roasted buckwheat
2½ cups (590 ml) defatted, low-sodium chicken stock
salt, optional
pepper, to taste
½ lb (230 g) smoked turkey sausage, diced
¾ cup (180 ml) diced cooked chicken
½ cup (120 ml) diced lean cooked ham
2 tbs (30 ml) chopped parsley
4-6 tbs (60-90 ml) low-fat plain yogurt
parsley sprigs, to garnish

Soak top and bottom of 3-quart (3 l) clay pot in water about 10 minutes; drain.

Heat oil in a small saucepan. Add the onion and garlic, cook for 2 minutes, then stir in the apricots and sultanas. Cook for another 2 minutes.

Place the buckwheat in the presoaked clay pot, add the onion mixture and pour in the stock. Add seasoning and stir well.

Cover the clay pot and place in a cold oven. Set oven at 425°F (220°C). Cook for 20 minutes. Sprinkle with the turkey sausage, chicken and ham and cook, covered, for another 10 minutes. Remove from heat and leave to stand, without removing the lid, for 10 minutes.

Fork the meat and parsley into the buckwheat and serve topped with the yogurt. Garnish with parsley. Serves 4 as substantial side dish.

Approximate nutritional analysis per serving:
Calories 519, Protein 41 g, Carbohydrates 61 g, Fat 13 g, Saturated Fat 4 g,
23% of Calories from Fat, Cholesterol 96 mg, Sodium 762 mg

Sprinkle with the turkey sausage, chicken and ham.

DESSERTS

APPLE-APRICOT SURPRISE

1 lb (455 g) cooking apples, peeled, cored and sliced
¼ cup (60 ml) superfine sugar
½ lb (230 g) ready-to-eat dried apricots, roughly chopped
2 tbs (30 ml) slivered almonds
½ cup (120 ml) evaporated skim milk, well chilled
dash vanilla

Soak top and bottom of 3-quart (3 l) clay pot in water about 10 minutes; drain.

Layer the apples, sugar and apricots in the presoaked clay pot. Cover the clay pot and place in a cold oven. Set oven at 425°F (220°C). Cook for 40 minutes or until apples are soft.

Sprinkle the almonds over the top and cook for another 5-10 minutes.
Whip evaporated skim milk with vanilla until stiff.

Serve whipped topping with warm apples. Serves 4.

Note: Without the apricots, the plain stewed apples may be beaten until smooth to make apple sauce. Chopped walnuts or crumbled chocolate wheat meal biscuits may be sprinkled over the apples instead of the slivered almonds.

Approximate nutritional analysis per serving:
Calories 230, Protein 5 g, Carbohydrates 51 g, Fat 3 g, Saturated Fat <1 g,
10% of Calories from Fat, Cholesterol 1 mg, Sodium 41 mg

Peel, core and slice the apples.

ONE-CRUST APPLE PIE

1⅓ cups (320 ml) sifted cake flour
1 tbs (15 ml) plus 1 tsp (5 ml) sugar
1½ tsp (8 ml) baking powder
4 tbs (60 ml) margarine or butter
1½-3 tbs (25-45 ml) ice water
2 lbs (910 g) cooking apples, peeled, cored and sliced
4 tbs (60 ml) raisins
grated rind and juice of 1 orange
4-6 cloves
skim milk, to glaze
superfine sugar, to glaze

Soak top and bottom of 3-quart (3 l) clay pot in water about 10 minutes; drain.

Using knife blade in food processor bowl, add the first three ingredients. Cover and process, pulsing 3 or 4 times or until combined. Add margarine or butter to flour mixture and pulse 5 or 6 times until mixture resembles coarse meal and is pale yellow. With the processor running, slowly add ice water, 1 tablespoon at a time. Process only until dough begins to form a ball and leaves sides of bowl.

Between two sheets of wax paper or heavy duty plastic that will be large enough for the final crust, form a rectangle, approximately 4x6 inches (10x15 cm), and refrigerate for 30 minutes.

Meanwhile, layer the apples, sugar and raisins in the presoaked clay pot; sprinkle the orange rind and juice between the layers, add the cloves somewhere about the middle of the filling.

Roll out the dough (still in the paper or plastic) 2 inches (5 cm) larger than the clay pot. Place in freezer approximately 10 minutes or until it is easy to peel off the paper and plastic. Trim 1 inch (2.5 cm) off the dough, then dampen the rim of the clay pot and press the dough trimmings on it. Dampen the dough rim. Cover with the rolled-out dough and press the edges together. Flute the dough edge. Make a small hole in the middle, then glaze with milk and sprinkle with superfine sugar.

Place clay pot, uncovered, in a cold oven. Set the oven at 425°F (220°C). Cook for 30 minutes. Reduce the temperature to 325°F (165°C) and cook for another 10 minutes until the apples are tender. Serves 8.

Approximate nutritional analysis per serving:
Calories 224, Protein 3 g, Carbohydrates 41 g, Fat 6 g, Saturated Fat 1 g,
24% of Calories from Fat, Cholesterol 0 mg, Sodium 262 mg

Dampen the dough rim. Cover with the rolled-out dough; press the edges together.

BAKED APPLES

4 large cooking apples, cored
2 tbs (30 ml) brown sugar
1 tsp (5 ml) ground cinnamon
4 tbs (60 ml) mixed dried fruit
grated rind and juice of 1 orange
2 tsp (10 ml) melted butter
½ cup (120 ml) evaporated skim milk, well chilled
¼ tsp (1 ml) vanilla

Soak top and bottom of 3-quart (3 l) clay pot in water about 10 minutes; drain.

Score the skin around the apples, check that all the core is removed from the middle of the fruit and that they stand neatly. Place a piece of nonstick baking parchment in the bottom of the presoaked clay pot, then stand the apples on it.

Mix together the brown sugar, cinnamon, dried fruit, orange rind and juice. Press this mixture into the core holes in the apples. Spoon the orange juice over, then drizzle the melted butter over.

Cover the clay pot and place in a cold oven. Set the oven at 475°F (246°C). Cook for 40-50 minutes or until the apples are tender but not collapsed. The time varies according to the size and particular type of apple, so check at 40-45 minutes. Whip evaporated skim milk with vanilla until stiff.

Serve whipped topping immediately with baked apples. Serves 4.

Approximate nutritional analysis per serving:
Calories 152, Protein 3 g, Carbohydrates 32 g, Fat 2 g, Saturated Fat 1 g,
13% of Calories from Fat, Cholesterol 6 mg, Sodium 37 mg

Mixed dried fruit makes an unusual stuffing.

BANANAS SUPREME

4 large firm bananas
juice of 1 lemon
3 tbs (45 ml) brown sugar
4 tsp (20 ml) butter
4 tbs (60 ml) brandy
4 tbs (60 ml) chopped mixed candied fruit, such as raisins,
  cherries or cranberries
½ cup (120 ml) evaporated skim milk
vanilla

Soak top and bottom of 3-quart (3 l) clay pot in water about 10 minutes; drain.

Halve the bananas lengthwise, place in the presoaked clay pot and sprinkle with the lemon juice. Top with brown sugar and dot with the butter.

Cover the clay pot and place in a cold oven. Set oven at 425°F (220°C). Cook for 30-35 minutes or until the sugar has melted and the bananas are hot and juicy. Pour the brandy over and set it alight.

When the flames have subsided, transfer the bananas to serving plates and top with candied fruit. Whip evaporated skim milk with vanilla until stiff and serve with bananas. Serves 4.

Note: As an alternative to candied fruit, macerate assorted dried fruit in an additional 4 tbs (60 ml) brandy. Add dried fruit before setting bananas and brandy alight.

Approximate nutritional analysis per serving:
Calories 242, Protein 4 g, Carbohydrates 50 g, Fat 4 g, Saturated Fat 3 g,
16% of Calories from Fat, Cholesterol 12 mg, Sodium 43 mg

Halve the bananas lengthwise.

WINTER FRUIT COMPOTE

1 lb (455 g) mixed dried fruit
4 cups (960 ml) red wine
2 cardamom pods
1 cinnamon stick
pared rind and juice of 1 orange
4 tbs (60 ml) brandy
2-4 tbs (30-60 ml) clear honey

Soak top and bottom of 3-quart (3 l) clay pot in water about 10 minutes; drain.

Place the fruit in a bowl. Pour in the wine and, if necessary, add just enough water to cover fruit. Cover and leave overnight.

Turn the fruit into the presoaked clay pot with all the soaking liquid. Add the cardamom pods and cinnamon, then stir in the orange juice. Shred half the rind finely and add it to the fruit.

Cover the clay pot and place in a cold oven. Set oven at 375°F (190°C). Cook for 1 hour, or until the fruit and rind are tender.

Stir in the brandy and honey to taste before serving. This compote is also good cold. Serves 8.

Approximate nutritional analysis per serving:
Calories 198, Protein 2 g, Carbohydrates 45 g, Fat <1 g, Saturated Fat <1 g,
2% of Calories from Fat, Cholesterol 0 mg, Sodium 4 mg

Dried fruit with brandy and honey.

SWEET AND SOUR COMPOTE

2 lbs (910 g) tender rhubarb, trimmed
¹/₂ cup (120 ml) superfine sugar
¹/₂ tsp (3 ml) fresh grated ginger
1 14-oz can (420 g) green figs in syrup
6 small sprigs mint

Soak top and bottom of 3-quart (3 l) clay pot in water about 10 minutes; drain.

Cut the rhubarb into 2-inch (5 cm) lengths, then place them in the presoaked clay pot with the sugar and ginger. Drain the canned figs and pour the syrup over the rhubarb.

Cover the clay pot and place in a cold oven. Set oven at 425°F (220°C). Cook for 40 minutes or until the rhubarb is tender but not mushy. The cooking time will vary; older thick rhubarb takes longer than tender young fruit.

Gently mix the figs and 2 of the mint sprigs with the rhubarb and cook, covered, for 5 minutes to heat the figs and give the compote a refreshing mint taste.

Decorate individual portions with a mint sprig when serving. Serves 6.

Approximate nutritional analysis per serving:
Calories 154, Protein 2 g, Carbohydrates 39 g, Fat <1 g, Saturated Fat <1 g,
2% of Calories from Fat, Cholesterol 0 mg, Sodium 7 mg

Cut the rhubarb into 2-inch lengths.

SUMMERTIME COBBLER

1 lb (455 g) blackberries
⅔ cup (160 ml) superfine sugar, plus extra for sprinkling
5 fresh peaches, blanched, peeled and pitted
1 cinnamon stick
1½ cups (355 ml) self-rising flour
3 tbs (45 ml) butter or margarine
½ cup (120 ml) skim milk, approximately
a little lemon juice

Soak top and bottom of 3-quart (3 l) clay pot in water about 10 minutes; drain.

Place the blackberries and ½ cup (120 ml) of the sugar in the presoaked clay pot. Slice 3 of the peaches; reserve the last for garnish. Add the rest to the clay pot with the cinnamon stick. Mix the fruit together.

Cover the clay pot and place in a cold oven. Set oven at 425°F (220°C). Cook for 40 minutes or until the blackberries are cooked.

Place the flour in a bowl and cut in the shortening. Mix in the remaining sugar and enough milk to make a soft dough. Knead just enough to combine. Roll out thickly and cut out 1½-inch (3.75 cm) round biscuits. Overlap these on top of the fruit. Brush with milk and sprinkle with sugar, then cook, uncovered, for another 15-20 minutes or until the biscuits are cooked.

Slice the remaining peach into very thin pieces, toss with lemon juice, then use to decorate the cooked cobbler. Serves 8.

Approximate nutritional analysis per serving:
Calories 243, Protein 4 g, Carbohydrates 48 g, Fat 5 g, Saturated Fat 3 g,
17% of Calories from Fat, Cholesterol 12 mg, Sodium 306 mg

Mix the different fruits in the clay pot.

BREADS

RYE BREAD WITH WILD SEED MIX

2 pkgs active dry yeast or 1 oz (30 g) fresh yeast
¾ cup (180 ml) lukewarm water
¼ cup (60 ml) molasses
1½ tbs (25 ml) salt
3½ cups (840 ml) rye flour
3 tbs (45 ml) caraway seeds
1 tbs (15 ml) poppy seeds
1 tbs (15 ml) sesame seeds
1 tsp (5 ml) celery seeds
¾ cup (180 ml) lukewarm buttermilk
1 egg, beaten
2 tbs (30 ml) melted butter
2 cups (480 ml) all-purpose flour
oil for bowl and clay pot

Combine the yeast, lukewarm water, molasses and salt. Set aside to allow the yeast to dissolve. Combine the rye flour and all the seeds in a large mixing bowl. In a separate bowl, combine the buttermilk, beaten egg and melted butter, then add to the rye flour-seed mixture. Add the yeast mixture, then add the all-purpose flour

Knead the mixture on a floured counter or bread board until smooth and elastic, then place the dough in a large oiled bowl. Cover with a damp cloth and allow to rise in a warm place for about 2 hours or until the dough doubles in bulk.

When the rising time is about over, presoak a 4¾-quart (4.6 l) clay pot, top and bottom, in water about 10 minutes; drain. Punch the dough down and reshape it into one round loaf. Place a small piece of nonstick baking parchment on the bottom of the presoaked clay pot to prevent sticking, oil the sides; then place the dough in the pot, cover and allow to rise in a warm place for about 1 hour or until doubled in bulk. Cover the clay pot and place in a cold oven. Set oven at 475°F (245°C). Bake for 55 minutes, removing the lid for the last 5 minutes to brown the crust. Yields 1 large loaf or 24 slices.

Approximate nutritional analysis per slice:
Calories 119, Protein 3 g, Carbohydrates 23 g, Fat 2 g, Saturated Fat <1 g,
14% of Calories from Fat, Cholesterol 12 mg, Sodium 149 mg

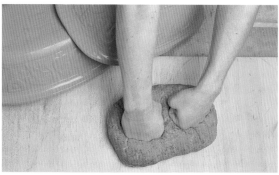

Knead the mixture on a floured bread board until smooth and elastic

ONION DILL BREAD

1 ¼ cup (295 ml) lukewarm water
1 tsp (5 ml) salt
1 tbs (15 ml) chopped fresh dillweed
large pinch of powdered saffron
1 pkg active dry yeast
4 cups (960 ml) sifted all-purpose flour
2 tbs (30 ml) olive oil
1 onion, choppd fine
¼ green pepper, chopped fine
1 ½ tbs (25 ml) butter
oil for bowl and clay pot

In a large metal bowl, combine the lukewarm water, salt, dillweed, saffron and yeast (crumbling it until well dissolved). Keep the metal bowl lukewarm so the yeast stays active.

Sift the flour into a large bowl and make a well in the center. Pour the yeast mixture into the well; stir, then knead the dough with your hands for about 10 minutes or until the dough is smooth and elastic. Pour the olive oil over the dough and knead for about 5 minutes, until it is no longer sticky. Put the dough in a large oiled bowl, cover with a towel and set in a warm place until the dough doubles. When the rising time is about over, presoak a 3 quart (3 l) clay pot, top and bottom, in water for 10 minutes; drain.

Sauté the onion and green pepper in the butter until tender but not browned, then remove the pan from the heat to cool. While it is cooling, roll the dough into an oblong shape ¼-inch (.625 cm) thick. Sprinkle the onion and green pepper mixture over the dough and fold in half lengthwise. Cut dough into three long strips and braid into a loaf.

Place a piece of nonstick baking parchment in the bottom of the presoaked clay pot. Oil the sides. Place the braided loaf in the clay pot, cover with lid, and let rise in a warm place until doubled in size, about 60 minutes. Cover the clay pot and place it in a cold oven. Set the oven at 450°F (230°C). Bake for 45 minutes, then remove the pot from the the oven and check bread for doneness. Return the pot to the oven, uncovered, and brown for additional 15 minutes. Bread will be done when a finger thump on the loaf's surface sounds hollow.

Allow bread to cool for 15-20 minutes before serving. Yields 1 loaf or 12 slices.

Approximate nutritional analysis per slice:
Calories 194, Protein 5 g, Carbohydrates 34 g, Fat 4 g, Saturated Fat 1 g,
19% of Calories from Fat, Cholesterol 4 mg, Sodium 180 mg

Cut dough into three long strips and braid into a loaf.

CARROT BREAD

1 ½ pkgs active dry yeast
    or ¾ oz (23 g) fresh yeast
¼ cup (60 ml) lukewarm water
3 ½-4 cups (840-960 ml) all-purpose flour
⅔ tsp (3 ml) salt
1 cup (240 ml) granulated sugar
½ cup (120 ml) brown sugar
2 eggs, beaten
2 cups (480 ml) shredded carrots
⅓ cup (80 ml) cooking oil
½ cup (120 ml) chopped walnuts
3 tbs olive oil

Dissolve the yeast in the lukewarm water and set aside.

In a large bowl, combine 3½ cups (840 ml) of the flour, salt and sugars. In a separate bowl, combine the beaten eggs, shredded carrots, cooking oil and chopped nuts. Mix well and add the flour along with the yeast mixture. Then knead into a round ball, using the remaining ½ cup (120 ml) flour, if necessary, to create an elastic nonsticky dough. Place the dough in an oiled bowl, cover with a damp cloth and set aside in a warm place to rise.

Just before rising time is over, soak 2 3-quart (3 l) clay pots, tops and bottoms, in water 10 minutes; drain.

Punch the dough down and reshape into 2 round loaves. Place a small piece of nonstick baking parchment on the bottom of each presoaked pot to prevent sticking. Oil the sides. Place the loaves in the pots, cover with the lids and allow to rise until nearly doubled in bulk.Place the covered clay pots in a cold oven. Set oven at 450°F (230°C). Bake for about 50 minutes, until a finger thump on the bread's surface sounds hollow. Yields 2 loaves or 24 slices.

Note: You can reserve half of the dough, covered in the refrigerator, if you want to bake only one loaf. You can bake the other loaf up to several days later.

Approximate nutritional analysis per slice:
Calories 171, Protein 3 g, Carbohydrates 29 g, Fat 5 g, Saturated Fat <1 g,
26% of Calories from Fat, Cholesterol 18 mg, Sodium 75 mg

Combine the beaten eggs, shredded carrots, oil and nuts.

BRAIDED BREAD

4 cups (960 ml) bread flour
1 tsp (5 ml) salt
2 tbs (30 ml) soft spread margarine
1 pkg active dry yeast
1 cup (120 ml) lukewarm skim milk, or water
1 beaten egg, to glaze
1 tbs (15 ml) poppy seeds
oil for bowl and clay pot

Soak top and bottom of 4¾-quart (4.6 l) clay pot in water about 10 minutes; drain. Line bottom with nonstick baking parchment and oil sides.

Place the flour and salt in a bowl. Cut in the margarine, then mix in the yeast. Mix in the 1 cup (240 ml) lukewarm skim milk or water to make a firm dough. Knead the dough for about 10 minutes, until it is smooth and elastic.

Divide the dough into thirds, then roll each piece into a long, thin rope. Attach the ropes of dough at one end, then braid them together into a wide plump braid.

Place the bread in the clay pot, plumping it neatly, then leave in a warm place until it has doubled in size. Brush with beaten egg and sprinkle with poppy seeds.

Cover the clay pot and place in a cold oven. Set oven at 450°F (230°C). Cook for 50 minutes. Uncover the pot and cook for another 10 minutes. Transfer to a wire rack to cool.

Yields 1 large loaf or 12 generous slices.

Approximate nutritional analysis per slice:
Calories 174, Protein 5 g, Carbohydrates 33 g, Fat 2 g, Saturated Fat <1 g,
12% of Calories from Fat, Cholesterol <1 mg, Sodium 208 mg

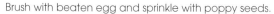

Brush with beaten egg and sprinkle with poppy seeds.

ZUCCHINI BREAD

1 ¾ cups (415 ml) all-purpose flour
2 tsp (10 ml) baking powder
½ tsp (3 ml) baking soda
¼ tsp (1 ml) salt
½ cup (120 ml) sugar
½ cup (120 ml) buttermilk
1 whole egg plus 1 egg white
2 tbs (30 ml) vegetable oil or melted butter
1 tsp (5 ml) vanilla, optional
    or ½ tsp (3 ml) lemon extract, optional
1 cup (240 ml) finely shredded zucchini
¾ cup (180 ml) golden raisins
1 tsp (5 ml) grated lemon rind
oil for the claypot

Soak top and bottom of 3-quart (3 l) clay pot in water about 10 minutes; drain and line with nonstick baking parchment. Oil the sides of the pot.

    In a large bowl, combine flour, baking powder, baking soda, salt and sugar. In another bowl, combine buttermmilk, egg, oil and vanilla or lemon extract. Squeeze the zucchini between paper towels to remove excess moisture. Stir zucchini, raisins and lemon rind into the buttermilk mixture. Pour liquid ingredients into dry. Mix just enough to moisten dry ingredients. Turn into the clay pot and smooth the top.

    Cover the clay pot and place in a cold oven. Set oven at 400°F (205°C). Cook for 1 hour. Uncover the clay pot and cook another 8-10 minutes for extra crispness. Insert a metal skewer into the bread: if it is sticky on the surface, the loaf is not cooked.

    Cool on a wire rack, serve sliced. Yields 1 large loaf or 12 slices.

Approximate nutritional analysis per serving:
Calories 190, Protein 4 g, Carbohydrates 32 g, Fat 5 g, Saturated Fat 2 g,
25% of Calories from Fat, Cholesterol 26 mg, Sodium 132 mg

Stir zucchini, raisins and lemon rind into buttermilk mixture.

HONEY WHOLE WHEAT BREAD

2 cups (480 ml) whole wheat flour
¼ cup (60 ml) nonfat dry milk
1½ tsp (8 ml) salt
1 pkg active dry yeast
1¼ cups (295 ml) warm water (105-115-°F [41-46°C])
¼ cup (60 ml) honey
1 tbs (15 ml) vegetable oil
2 cups (480 ml) all-purpose flour, approximately
oil for bowl and clay pot

Combine whole wheat flour, dry milk, salt and yeast in large mixing bowl. Add warm water, honey and oil. Mix until blended; beat with wooden spoon for 3 minutes.

Mix in 1½ cups (355 ml) of the all-purpose flour to make stiff dough. Turn dough onto floured surface. Knead, adding flour as needed, until dough is smooth and elastic and small bubbles form just under surface, 15-20 minutes.

Place dough in an oiled bowl; turn oiled side up. Let stand covered in a warm place until doubled, about 1¼-1½ hours.

Soak top and bottom of a loaf-shaped, 5½-cup (1.3 l) clay pot in water about 15 minutes. When dough has doubled, drain bottom of clay pot; pat dry; oil sides and bottom generously.

Punch down dough; shape into oblong loaf and place in clay pot. Cover with waxed paper; let stand in warm place until dough nearly reaches top of clay pot, 25-30 minutes.

Drain top of clay pot; pat dry and oil.

Place covered clay pot in a cold oven. Set oven at 425°F (220°C). Bake until bread sounds hollow when tapped, 40-45 minutes. Remove cover; bake until top is dark brown, 2-4 minutes.

Remove from clay pot; cool on wire rack. Yields 1 loaf or 12 slices.

Approximate nutritional analysis per slice:
Calories 182, Protein 6 g, Carbohydrates 37 g, Fat 2 g, Saturated Fat <1 g,
8% of Calories from Fat, Cholesterol <1 mg, Sodium 187 mg

Punch down dough; shape into oblong loaf; place in clay pot.

FRENCH BREAD

1 ⅓ cups (320 ml) warm water (105-115°F (41-46°C))
1 pkg active dry yeast
1 tbs (15 ml) sugar
1 ½ tsp (8 ml) salt
1 tbs (15 ml) vegetable oil
4 cups (960 ml) all-purpose flour, approximately
oil for bowl and clay pot

This works best in an elongated clay pot designed for fish.

Place lukewarm water in large bowl; sprinkle with yeast. Let stand until yeast is dissolved, about 3 minutes. Stir in sugar, salt and oil. Add 2¾ cups (660 ml) of the flour. Mix until blended; beat with wooden spoon until dough is elastic and pulls away from bowl, about 5 minutes.

Add ¾ cup (180 ml) of the flour to make soft dough. Turn dough onto floured surface. Knead, adding additional flour as needed, until dough is smooth and springy and small bubbles form just under surface, 20-25 minutes.

Place dough in an oiled bowl; coat with oil and turn oiled side up. Let stand covered in warm place until doubled, 1-1½ hours.

Soak bottom of a loaf-shaped, 5½-cup (1.3 l) clay pot in water about 10 minutes or until rising time is up. When dough has doubled, drain bottom of clay pot; pat dry; oil sides and bottom. Punch down dough; shape into narrow loaf, about 11 inches (302.5 cm) long, and place in a clay pot. Cover with waxed paper and let stand in warm place until nearly doubled, about 45 minutes. Cut 3 diagonal slashes, 1-inch (2.5 cm) deep, in top of dough with razor blade or sharp knife.

Soak top of clay pot in water about 15 minutes; drain after loaf has finished second rising. Place covered clay pot in cold oven. Set oven at 475°F (246°C). Bake until bread sounds hollow when tapped, 45-50 minutes. Remove cover; bake until top is brown, 1-3 minutes.

Remove from clay pot; cool on wire rack. Yields 1 large loaf, or 12 slices.

Approximate nutritional analysis per slice:
Calories 167, Protein 5 g, Carbohydrates 33 g, Fat 2 g, Saturated Fat <1 g,
9% of Calories from Fat, Cholesterol 0 mg, Sodium 268 mg

Knead until
dough is
smooth and
springy and
small bubbles
form just
under
surface.

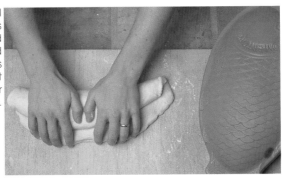